# Praise for

# *ELITE AND TRUE*

"I read *Elite and True* in just two days as I found it highly engaging and rewarding. One's destiny can be determined by a surprisingly small number of key life decisions—sometimes as few as one or two in a lifetime. So I enjoyed living alongside Barnhart day-to-day while he tenaciously pursued early acceptance into NUPOC, ostensibly to "just pay the bills," but leading him to learn what true leadership is and is not. He then parlayed those lessons into success in the high-tech business sector.

From the first page, I was instantly drawn into Barnhart's life story of leadership lessons—some learned straightforwardly; others the hard way. I found the book engaging and very much enjoyed Barnhart's down-to-earth writing style. I both grimaced and laughed out loud several times while reading! As someone who has personally worked alongside Barnhart in the business sector, I can attest to the authenticity and success of his leadership style as portrayed in *Elite and True*.

*Elite and True* is invaluable for someone making the transition from military service to the private sector. For that matter, for anyone who desires to transition from a career path not well suited to one better matched to their passions and career goals."

**—BOB AKINS,** co-founder, former CEO and Chairman, Cymer

# ELITE

### AND

# TRUE

# ELITE

## AND

# TRUE

LEADERSHIP LESSONS
INSPIRED BY THE US NAVY

## JAMES L. BARNHART

GREENLEAF
BOOK GROUP PRESS

Published by Greenleaf Book Group Press
Austin, Texas
www.gbgpress.com

Distributed by Greenleaf Book Group

For ordering information or special discounts for bulk purchases, please contact Greenleaf Book Group at PO Box 91869, Austin, TX 78709, 512.891.6100.

Design and composition by Greenleaf Book Group
Cover design by Greenleaf Book Group
Cover image courtesy of the Navy Exchange Service Command

Publisher's Cataloging-in-Publication data is available.

Print ISBN: 978-1-62634-968-1

eBook ISBN: 978-1-62634-969-8

Part of the Tree Neutral® program, which offsets the number of trees consumed in the production and printing of this book by taking proactive steps, such as planting trees in direct proportion to the number of trees used: www.treeneutral.com

Printed in the United States of America on acid-free paper

22 23 24 25 26 27 28 29   10 9 8 7 6 5 4 3 2 1

First Edition

To James Ace and Dennis Ray—role models of true leadership. Your influence is greater than you will ever know.

# CONTENTS

# INTRODUCTION

My working days started at an early age. While still in grammar school, I began working on a local farm, being paid by volume for picking strawberries and raspberries during the summer. Through middle school, I continued farm work during the summers and added daily newspaper delivery year-round. By high school, I had earned the experience and trust of the farmer to move from picking berries to working for hourly pay as field boss overseeing efficient and effective field harvesting, and to harvesting corn, potatoes, and hot-house rhubarb. This expanded the work from a seasonal summer job to weekend and school-break employment through the fall and into the winter.

The days were long. I came to appreciate the cool morning air during the six o'clock hour before the summer sun began its relentless march across the southern sky. The humidity in the well-irrigated fields was high, as midday temperatures frequently hovered in the 80s with an occasional burst up to triple digits Fahrenheit. When the farm workday ended and my field mates headed home, I headed to my newspaper route to deliver the afternoon edition before meeting up with cross-country teammates for a training run.

Physical fitness came with the work. The modest lifestyle farm depended upon manual labor for most operations. Harvesting berries required reaching from ground level with strawberries to overhead and anywhere in between with raspberries. The full "flats" of berries—wooden crates with a dozen waxed-paper boxes used for harvesting berries bound for cannery processing—added weight quickly, and stacking them onto the flatbed truck where they would tower up to a height of five feet required repeated climbing up and down. Corn harvesting involved removing ears from stalks, counting a gross of ears into waxed cardboard boxes, and stacking the packed boxes onto the flatbed truck for transport to market. Potato harvesting required picking up from the soil the spuds unearthed by a mechanical digger and placing them into burlap sacks. The full sacks weighed up to 100 lbs. and had to be manually lifted onto the three-foot-high field truck bed.

Eight hours of farm work followed by a bicycle ride to the newspaper pick-up point, stuffing the papers into a heavy canvas double-pouch carrier bag, wrestling the loaded bag over my head for balanced front-back shoulder carry, then trudging door-to-door for the two-mile circuit of the newspaper delivery route built muscle and discipline.

On top of that, customer feedback built character. With area rainfall exceeding 45 inches in an average year, each home-delivery customer had a preferred delivery spot for the newspaper where it would stay dry and where they could most readily retrieve it without getting doused themselves. To accumulate nearly four feet of water annually, the weather was inclement nine months of the year, ranging from an annoying drizzle to what my father called a "frog-strangling downpour" interspersed with an occasional snowfall during the winter. On one particularly obnoxious day, large raindrops pounded off the pavement and bounced back up to knee height. As I opened the stormproof screen door to sandwich the rolled newspaper between that and the front door—the specified delivery requirement for this house—an elderly lady swung open the front door to my surprise. With piercing eyes and a harsh tone, she snatched the paper from my hand and demanded, "Have you ever tried to read a wet newspaper?" She berated me for more than a minute, complaining about the paper being too wet in recent days and how she could even see my wet fingerprints on today's front page. As I stood in the torrential downpour taking in her feedback, water streaming down my face, droplets sequentially rolling from my fingertips to join those bouncing back up from her porch, I apologized. I committed to pulling her paper from the middle of the stack in the days ahead, which would lessen the moisture absorbed from the saturated canvas bag slung over my shoulders. As character-building as daily newspapers delivery could be, the monthly collection cycle could prove just as entertaining. My knock on the door was often followed by shushing sounds inside the home and occupants telling one another to keep quiet until the paperboy-come-to-collect moved on to the next home.

Time for introspection abounded as I went about my day's work. The many hours trudging in the rain, snow, or even in the blazing sun to deliver newspapers gave me ample time to ponder my career path. The hours toiling in the farmer's field, hoeing weeds when not harvesting crops, added to my thinking time. I was tallying the pros and cons of studying to be a veterinarian late one hot summer afternoon while hoeing weeds from rows of immature strawberry plants when a commotion arose. The farm had recently suffered a break to an irrigation line buried underground at the intersection of two dirt access roads, and the force of escaping water had eroded a pit six feet across and four feet deep. A truck driver, who had just refreshed the portable toilets about the farm as his last stop at the end of a long day, had cut the corner too close and sunk his right rear axle into the pit. The twisted tipping of his full truck caused part of his tank load to spill into the pit. The farmer summoned me with a shovel to help dig out the true shithead driver.

Timing is everything.

Not long after I helped excavate the "sanitary" truck driver, my business-executive uncle phoned to inquire my interest in moving from outdoor farm work in dreary Washington State to an indoor stint in sunny California. Trading field labor with a hoe for indoor work with a computer was an easy decision for a high school kid. It would be hard to leave my friends and teammates in Washington, but it would only be for the summer and I could continue my training for the upcoming cross-country season in the San Francisco Bay Area. Uncle had arranged everything for a successful summer internship, from securing a job with the warehouse team at Commodore Business Machines to clearing a bedroom in his house and allowing me to ride to and from work with him. I happily accepted his kind offer and flew to San Jose for the balance of the summer break.

Warehouse work was enlightening. An experienced coworker walked me through the receiving process, explaining how to populate the pertinent data fields in the inventory control database, and where to route the materials that needed quality inspection separate from those that went directly to stock. Toward the end of the quarter, the shipments increased and I moved to the shipping area to package computers and load outbound trucks. As labor demand across departments ebbed and flowed, I learned the work across multiple areas and floated to wherever I was most needed. The work was educational and fun, as I met new people and learned both new products and new processes. As my competence increased, my supervisor enjoyed my contributions. Tasks that had been the purview of his role, he began assigning to me. It was a win-win situation; he gained free time while I learned new things. As he learned he could rely on me for coverage, however, he began to take more frequent breaks and to leave earlier for lunch and to return a bit later in the afternoon. He may have been an adequate supervisor, assigning tasks and seeing that work was completed by subordinates, but he was not much of a leader. He provided no inspiration and slacked off when the opportunity presented itself.

Conversations with my uncle that summer were more inspiring. On our morning and evening commutes together we discussed an incredible range of topics, from the mundane activities of the day to the thought-provoking questions about life. What career path would I pursue? How did he come to be vice president for marketing and sales at Commodore? Through our discussions, I became convinced that microelectronics would be the future and that I would study electrical engineering after high school.

Our conversations grew more profound through time. Uncle was CEO of Eagle Computer when he offered me a similar internship arrangement as an engineering technician the summer after my sophomore year of college. One sunny afternoon as we drove home from the office, he shared his vision for where he would take the company. Impressed, I could not help but ask, "Where do you get the confidence?" He burst into hearty laughter before explaining a fact that I had never pondered before and that I struggled to believe at the time: Most people want to be led! Bring forward a vision for a better future and people will gladly follow.

I did not truly appreciate this pearl of wisdom at the time but I had the good fortune to have outstanding leadership role models within my immediate family. My father, James Ace Barnhart, and my aforementioned uncle, Dennis Ray Barnhart, pursued distinctly different career paths in public service and in corporate business, respectively. They both rose to lead their chosen organizations to excellence. Other than the two being brothers, the common denominator to their leadership success and their career launching point was their training in the United States Navy.

The USN instilled in them the principles of discipline, teamwork, physical fitness, and leadership that launched their civilian careers after separation from military service. James, a radioman, became a civilian firefighter who demonstrated determination and discipline while earning promotions to captain, assistant chief, municipal fire marshal, and chief. He adhered to existing codified rules in the early days, then drafted new ones to enable firefighting and emergency response to grow to accommodate population and jurisdiction expansions. Dennis, an aviator, took an entrepreneurial path, developing products ranging from saltwater aquariums to calculators, handheld electronic games and personal computers. Both these role models observed elements in their surroundings that could or should be improved upon, then set about effecting the desired changes.

When deciding my own education and career path, I chose a blend influenced by both their leads, completing studies in electrical engineering before joining the USN's elite Nuclear Propulsion Officer Candidate program and pursuing service aboard a nuclear submarine. *Elite and True* is the story of my experiences during seven years of naval service and my transition to corporate America's executive career track with a personal distillation of lessons collected along the way. It chronicles my growth through four stages, from an unsure follower in Part I to a determined follower in Part II, to a positional leader in Part III, and finally a true leader in Part IV. Each piece of leadership advice derives from a real-world situation I faced, which I share in experiential form before contextualizing it more generally in a leadership lesson at the end of each chapter for broader application to leadership situations elsewhere. Although the book's four parts follow the timeline of my personal journey, I encourage you to pull from the leadership lessons offered here in the order you deem most appropriate to your own leadership situation.

I believe the true leaders among us inspire others to perform at renewed levels. The true leader exudes passion, confidence, and intelligence that motivates others to follow, without relying upon a hierarchical title of a given position as the basis for authority to lead. To the subordinates bound by organizational hierarchy to do as directed by the positional leader, a true leader offers a refreshing change. People are drawn to a true leader, with or without a title that denotes a formal position.

Enjoy your journey toward increased productivity with strengthened workforce morale as you apply these elite (and true) leadership lessons.

# PART I

# UNSURE FOLLOWER

Where am I going? How will I get there? These two questions face each of us at various times in our lives. In the absence of clear answers to these personal questions, we might find ourselves simply going with the flow, following a path laid out by someone else. There is a certain comfort in following the leader, whether that leader be a buddy, a coach, a supervisor, or an employer company. All is well as long as the leader and our internal compass are aligned.

But when the path we are following seems uncertain, when we feel no particular passion as we journey, it is time for introspection. The answers to the two questions above will either confirm our current path to be sound, or provide needed motivation for a commitment to change.

# 1

# THE NUPOC PROGRAM

## LEADERSHIP LESSON 1.A.
## PERSISTENCE PAYS.

The ad was compelling. It was just one obscure little paragraph buried among the filler in the university campus daily rag. A thousand dollars per month for going to college and working toward an undergraduate degree. In 1981 dollars that was real money, and to a starving student pondering how he would afford tuition, books, and room and board next fall, one toll-free phone call certainly couldn't hurt. After all, I had been saving money for college since the seventh grade, doing farm work during the summer and delivering newspapers year-round. The years of savings were enough to cover freshman expenses with a remaining balance which, combined with yet another summer's toil in the fields, would barely cover the cost of a sophomore year. A third year was untenable at this rate, let alone the dream of funding a fourth year that would be required to earn a bachelor's degree. Yes, I would have to learn more about the Navy's NUPOC program.

The term NUPOC served as my indoctrination to the world of Navy acronyms. "NUclear Propulsion Officer Candidate," the recruiter cheerfully recited when I placed a tentative call. "But that program's not for you," he quickly added. "The NUPOC program is for students in their senior year. You're only a sophomore." I had rather expected him to jump at the chance to sign up another warm body, but he seemed downright anxious to get off the phone with me. So much for the recruiter stereotype. When I tried the same number two weeks later, the answer on NUPOC was the same. Although this time the enthusiastic recruiter tried to earn his keep by giving me a spiel on the merits of NROTC.

I knew several ROTC (Reserve Officer Training Corps) students. They were the clean-shaven ones with the buzz haircuts. They wore uniforms on campus and endured military history courses along with the normal classes for their chosen field of study. They marched and drilled and underwent inspections in those tidy uniforms. They also received $100 per month for their efforts—a nice way to defray pizza costs, but not a viable means of paying for an education. No, I wanted to learn more about the NUPOC program.

Ask and ye shall receive! Posted outside the campus chemistry labs, where only the dedicated or lost students could ever be expected to take notice, there was a colorful bill complete with tear-away information-request postcards proclaiming the wonders of the NUPOC program. I took a card, filled in the return address information, and dropped it in the mail while walking home from class that very same day.

The next week a recruiter called to inquire about my course of study and grades to date. During this conversation I learned that the typical NUPOC student was a college senior nearing graduation but there was also an "exceptional student" program for those who qualified after completing at least two years of technical course work. It required repeated requests on my part, but with sufficient pestering, the recruiter finally agreed to send me a package of information on the NUPOC program. No wonder they were so reluctant to advertise the comparative benefits of the NUPOC program. It carried a $6,000 signing bonus ($3,000 up front with the balance paid upon completion of training), it paid $1,000 per month for going to school, and neither uniforms nor military courses were required. As a NUPOC exceptional student, the only additional requirement would be to maintain better than a 3.33/4.0 grade point average while completing my desired technical undergraduate degree. The required six years of service seemed a significant commitment, but the fine print indicated that the clock started ticking at the time of sign-on. If I could get in at the earliest opportunity, at the completion of my sophomore year, I would receive two years' service credit just for completing my junior and senior years of college. An additional year after that would be consumed by required nuclear training before I ever served any actual time in the fleet. Compared with the ROTC four-year commitment after graduation, the NUPOC program was clearly the better solution to my financial dilemma.

Life choices are rarely so simple as a financial analysis of two mutually exclusive alternatives. What about finding a part-time job to work my way through school instead? I knew several people who had taken this path, none of whom had even come close to paying their student debts, however, and their studies and overall college experience had suffered from the chronic workload overextension. What if I took a year or two off from school to earn enough money to finance the balance of my education? I had other friends who had opted for this approach. Unfortunately, the graduation rate of those who took time off school was notably lower than those who tried to work their way straight through with no appreciable gap between academic sessions. Most of my acquaintances who "took a year off" never quite got around to going back to school to finish their degrees. Whether it be the satisfaction of landing a respectable hourly position or life's call to form a family and the pursuit of happiness, the perils of taking a sabbatical from college seemed too great.

There was also the consideration of military duty. The Cold War was in full swing and the nation in general didn't look favorably upon military service and those in uniform. Movies such as *The Deer Hunter* and *Apocalypse Now* were solid indicators of the national psyche. Works like

*Top Gun* and Tom Clancy's patriotic writings that glamorize military service were yet to come. Even if I could set aside the public's disdain for the military and proudly serve my country, would I really want to work directly on, around, and with nuclear power? Could I see myself locked in a submarine reliant upon nuclear energy for survival? After some serious soul-searching and numerous discussions with family and friends, I decided that the NUPOC program was the right answer. Nuclear power seemed like a worthy intellectual challenge, and I decided that if my father and uncle made it through their time of service, that I also would prevail. Plus, I needed the money.

Through all of this soul searching, the possibility that the Navy might not actually want another NUPOC was the least of my worries. After all, these were lean times for recruiters and I had the science and technical studies background described in their literature. The trouble was, the recruiters seemed eager to talk about ROTC, but they became reticent whenever I brought up the NUPOC program, especially that little exceptional student clause. They clearly considered my questions to be a waste of their time. They did not expect that I would be able to meet the stringent selection criteria, preferring to quote an acceptance rate of fewer than 3 percent rather than encouraging me to formally apply.

As it turned out, a student in the class ahead of me had applied for the NUPOC program and a recruiter was planning a trip to campus to meet with him and to obtain a copy of his transcript. With a bit more persistence, I was able to convince the recruiter to also meet with me and to accept a copy of my transcript during his visit. Shortly after our meeting, the recruiter telephoned to say that I had been invited to Washington, D.C., for NUPOC interviews, including a session with Admiral McKee, who was carrying on the tradition of recently retired Admiral Rickover by personally approving every officer in the nuclear Navy. Now we were making progress.

## LEADERSHIP LESSON 1.B.
## COMMIT YOURSELF.

Never having previously interviewed for any position, none of the NUPOC candidates knew what to expect. On the eve of our scheduled interviews, we were paired up in a local Arlington, Virginia, hotel and told when to be ready in the lobby for the morning sessions at Naval Reactors. My assigned roommate was quite the global traveler, or so he fancied. He viewed the impending technical interviews as little more than a formality; they would likely request his services as an instructor for the nuclear training program, or so he believed. Maybe I should listen to him, I thought. He did seem to be a savvy traveler. The confidence he exuded in grabbing that small, thick towel from the bathroom rack and tossing it on the floor at the foot of the tub before showering was reassuring. Who would ever have guessed the hotel put such a towel there specifically for that purpose?

We must have been quite the sight on interview morning, each dressed in our finest department store polyester suit. Those of us who had lacked the foresight to pack a clip-on version of a tie were wrestling with striped polyester ties in an effort to display a presentable knot. Adrenaline and pulse rates were already running high when a lieutenant arrived at the hotel lobby to escort us to the interview site a few blocks away. I appreciated the oppressive June weather in Washington, D.C., even more than my perspiring compatriots, since I had truly gone all out and donned a three-piece suit, complete with matching polyester vest. When combined with my permanent pressed polyester mix shirt and tight necktie, the whole get-up effectively formed a hermetic seal over my sweating body. The walk may have been only a few blocks, but by the time we reached our destination, the wet sauna inside my suit made it apparent that this would be a long day.

Once comfortably inside the air-conditioned confines of the interview building, we received a briefing on the day's agenda.

We were to wait patiently in a community staging area filled with folding metal chairs until instructed otherwise. We would each be notified where to go when it was time for our interview, we would each have several interviews, and we were to follow the prescribed protocol in moving about the building and in introducing ourselves to the interviewers. The discussions would be technical in nature. Subject matter from any course reflected on our college transcripts, a copy of which had been delivered in advance to the interviewers, would be fair game for questions.

We were not to discuss the content of these interviews with each other during any of our communal waiting time between individual interview sessions.

My first interviewer noted that I had declared an electrical engineering major and he was interested to see what knowledge I had retained from physics. Handing me pen and paper, he asked that I outline Newton's laws of motion, describing the workings behind both the laws and my thinking as I wrote. It was difficult to read the stone-faced, facts-only interviewer, but things seemed to be going reasonably well when he asked me to explain how and why a siphon works. Drawings and commentary were insufficient; he wanted to see equations to back up the physical phenomena that I described. Walking in a mental haze along the polished corridors back to the group waiting room following that inaugural interview, I reflected longingly on that lovely open-air stroll we had taken earlier that morning.

After an uncomfortably long idle period in the communal waiting room that allowed an active, overly critical mind to regurgitate and critique in painful detail every moment of the preceding interview, the time came for my next ordeal. The next interviewer skimmed from subject to subject long enough to build up my confidence. His smile seemed to confirm that each answer I provided was correct. We had seemingly established a solid rapport by the time he asked me to "derive the area of a circle using integral calculus." Perhaps a bit giddy with my recent success in this session, I cockily attempted a strategic maneuver. Doing my best to deliver a tone that would lead him to conclude such a derivation between us friends would be too trivial for me to complete and for him to witness, I inquired, "In polar or rectangular coordinates?" Rather than recognizing my brilliance and moving to another question, he called my bluff with a wry smile and simply responded, "Both." Knowing that the formula for the area of a circle is $\pi r^2$ probably aided my effort as I miraculously wrote out and explained the derivation first in polar coordinates, then in rectangular. He had no further questions, nor did I.

Later in the prolonged afternoon, a third technical interviewer thoroughly tested my education to that point in electrical engineering. Satisfied with my answers to a battery of circuit theory and power delivery questions, he asked what seemed a disarmingly simple question. Observing the pages of scrawling that comprised my answers to his previous queries, he pointed out that in every circuit there were inefficiencies; in every case there was more power delivered than was put to intended use. His question was, where does that additional power go? When I answered that the majority of the missing power is dissipated as resistive heating loss, he erupted in joy, or at least expressed as much enthusiasm as one could expect from a tenured scientist. Apparently, he had been asking that question all day long and no one else had offered the correct answer. We spent the balance of the session talking like old friends about my studies and the importance of obtaining a well-rounded education rather than insisting on a parochial focus in any one discipline.

At the conclusion of the technical interview batteries, all the weary candidates regrouped in the community waiting room for one more test, the much anticipated and equally dreaded culmination of the entire selection process. The next step was the admiral's interview. The recruiters had warned us about this "interview." Admiral Rickover's antics in testing the mettle of his candidates were legendary. He would test the composure, the resolve, and the spirit of candidates by putting them through impromptu psychological trials.

By one storied account, the admiral noted that a candidate was engaged to be married. Commenting that this young man could take only one wife, Adm. Rickover challenged the candidate to decide whether he would wed his fiancée or the nuclear Navy, which would fully consume any man worthy of the challenge. After a few tense, ponderous moments, the candidate declared that the nuclear program was his choice. The admiral then offered the quivering lad a telephone and instructed him to call his fiancée on the spot to cancel their engagement. One can only imagine the pathetic performance of that impressionable fool as he stammered his way through an apologetic annulment of his engagement, explaining to his fiancée how he could take only one wife and that she was to be the nuclear Navy. Upon completion of the call, Adm. Rickover berated the spineless wimp for compromising himself in such a disgraceful manner and declared the candidate unsuitable for service in the nuclear Navy.

Another legend had a candidate seated in front of Adm. Rickover's desk when the admiral looked at the young man and challenged, "Make me mad." Incredulous, the candidate inquiringly repeated the order as he thought he heard it, only to receive a now emphatic and stern confirmation, "Make me mad!" Looking quickly about the office, the candidate could not help but fixate on the admiral's prized model of the USS *Nautilus*, handcrafted to exacting scale detail with a cutaway hull that displayed with exquisite accuracy the admiral's prized nuclear reactor plant. Without further hesitation the candidate smashed the model with his balled fist. Adm. Rickover curtly confirmed the candidate's acceptance into the nuclear program and ordered him out of the office.

Given the recent change in command, no one knew what to expect from Adm. McKee during these interviews. The admiral had been briefed on each candidate's performance that day, and his questions would likely be very direct to help him form a final decision on who would serve in his nuclear Navy and who would go home in rejection. When my time arrived, a nervous junior officer serving as the admiral's aide escorted me into the admiral's office in a smart manner and curtly introduced me, then hurriedly instructed me to be seated in the single chair directly in front of Adm. McKee's desk. Reading from my open file, Adm. McKee glanced at me over the top of the folder and asked, "Why do you want into this program?"

I replied matter-of-factly, "I need the money for school."

"Have you thought beyond school, to actual service in the fleet?" he continued.

"Of course I have, and I would serve my country with pride."

"What do your parents think about all this?" he challenged.

"It would ultimately be my decision, but my father and uncle both served in the Navy and my mother could best be described as worried but proud," I explained.

Just that fast, the admiral's aide was thanking the admiral and whisking me out of his office and back to the candidates' waiting room. In the end, six of us from the 22 who ran the interview gauntlet that day were selected for admission into the NUPOC program. After signing reams of paperwork, we received our first installment of the sign-on bonus money and had our photographs taken for our military identification cards. We were now official members of the US Navy.

After the brief stay in D.C., I returned to my normal summer job in preparation for the upcoming academic year. By the time fall rolled around, I returned to campus comfortable in the knowledge that my education was financially secure. Combining the sign-on bonus and monthly checks from the NUPOC program with my pay from three months of summer employment, I had saved $10,000 from spring final exam week to fall class enrollment.

## LEADERSHIP LESSON 1.C.
## MOST THINGS IN LIFE ARE NEGOTIABLE.

Junior year went according to plan. I took the normal undergraduate electrical engineering course load, collected my monthly NUPOC checks, and submitted my transcripts to the recruiter's office to prove that I was upholding my end of the Faustian bargain. Other than eating somewhat better than the typical poor student that I had been during the freshman and sophomore sessions, the year was uneventful.

Senior year proved to be much more interesting. I was enjoying my studies and continuing to earn solid marks in all courses when my university guidance counselor intimated that a few select students were being offered an opportunity to enroll in graduate courses that would earn them credit toward a graduate degree even while they were still finishing their undergraduate educations. The opportunity provided, in essence, the chance to earn a master's degree with just one year of additional study. The participants could even earn a little extra cash serving as a teacher's aide for underclassmen. The TA money held little allure at that time thanks to the generosity of the NUPOC program, but the thought of earning a master's degree in only one more year sure sounded like a great opportunity.

With fair excitement, I phoned the Navy recruiter to share my good fortune. I might as well have been talking to a wall, and an irritated one at that. Yes, I had signed a contract stating that upon successful completion of my bachelor of science degree I would commence my military service. I had no intention of trying to renege on that contract or breaking any other commitments. I was merely suggesting that my service date be postponed for one calendar year while I completed an additional course of study. I even expected suspension of my NUPOC pay and benefits during this time, too. By simply delaying things one year, the Navy would be getting someone with an MSEE rather than a BSEE. This was the very definition of win-win, right? But something about quotas and training pipelines seemed to get in the way of common sense, and I was forced to reluctantly decline the enticing offer from my alma mater.

COMMANDER
NAVY RECRUITING COMMAND

**3 0 MAR 1984**

Dear Mr. Barnhart,

Congratulations on your continued superior academic performance since your interview at Naval Reactors for participation in the Naval Nuclear Propulsion Program upon graduation.

At the time of your interview, there were only two programs available for exceptional students: a fleet assignment or instructor duty at Orlando, Florida. Now that you are within a year of graduation and because of your sustained academic performance, you are eligible for consideration as a junior engineer on Admiral McKee's staff at Naval Reactors Headquarters in the Washington, D. C. area.

This Headquarters engineering assignment is best suited for those who have not committed themselves to a career in the nuclear Navy but who are interested in duty involving both the technical and management aspects of engineering. Duty on Admiral McKee's staff is an extremely valuable experience for those who want to enter civilian industry after their first tour or for those who may want to stay at Naval Reactors as civilians or engineering duty officers upon completion of their four-year obligations. At Naval Reactors, you would be working for and with a very talented group of senior engineers who have been involved in the heart of the Naval Nuclear Propulsion Program for a number of years.

Enclosed is a brief list of questions and answers about work at Naval Reactors. After considering this offer carefully, it is requested that you contact your recruiter with any additional questions you may have and your final decision regarding this opportunity.

Volunteers are being solicited for a finite number of positions at Naval Reactors. The best qualified volunteers will be notified of their selection for interview.

Again Mr. Barnhart, the Navy is pleased with your academic performance. I sincerely hope that you will consider favorably this new opportunity, but whatever your decision, I wish you the best of luck in your future endeavor.

Sincerely,

J. D. WILLIAMS
Rear Admiral, U. S. Navy

Copy to:
CO, NRD Seattle

Things got even more interesting during the spring of my senior year. I arrived home from class one afternoon to find a letter of congratulations from my recruiter. His higher-ups at the Navy Recruiting Command had apparently decided that it might be acceptable to deviate from the contracted training and service pipeline.

I did as requested and called my recruiter again to discuss this new opportunity. It seemed the new program was sufficiently unknown that the recruiter had to refer me to a district office out at Treasure Island, California. The knowledgeable expert there did a great job of comparing and contrasting what I needed to know. It was want of money that got me started with the nuclear Navy, and I saw no reason to change my decision criteria at that point. An itemized summary of first-year pay and benefits in this new Naval Reactors path totaled $19,491.60 while the submarine fleet assignment would pay $25,011.60. By the fourth year of service the Naval Reactors opportunity would be paying $31,638 compared to submarine fleet pay of $39,918. Once in possession of the financial facts, it seemed both the Navy and I would have the chance to deny the other an opportunity to deviate from our original contract.

## LEADERSHIP LESSONS:

**1.A.** Persistence pays. As President Calvin Coolidge said, "Nothing in the world can take the place of persistence. Talent will not; nothing is more common than unsuccessful men with talent. Genius will not; unrewarded genius is almost a proverb. Education will not; the world is full of educated derelicts. Persistence and determination alone are omnipotent."

I doggedly pursued the recruiters because I needed accession to the NUPOC exceptional student program so badly that there was no other option in my mind. I could not deviate from my goal, and so I persisted.

**1.B.** Commit yourself. Ask yourself how committed you are to achieving an objective. When you are certain you need it even more than you want it, write it down. Review your commitment regularly and pursue it with unwavering determination until you achieve it. You may be slowed or set back during your pursuit, but you cannot accept any outcome other than success.

Recruiter after recruiter tried to steer me away from the NUPOC program, but my commitment to securing a slot as a NUPOC led them to submit my credentials. Once invited for the interview process in D.C., I learned how to don a business suit and reminded myself while sitting in the waiting room why I had volunteered to run that interview gauntlet. I was committed to gaining entry into the NUPOC program as the most viable means of securing money needed to complete my college education.

**1.C.** Most things in life are negotiable. The trick is to prepare well for the negotiation. Before ever engaging the other party, be sure you will be meeting with the right, empowered representative. Know what you need and want from the negotiation, as well as what you are willing to concede. Make every effort to discern the same about those seated on the other side of the table and you will walk away with a desirable outcome nearly every time. Had I spoken to a senator or congressman rather than a recruiter whose performance was being measured on a quarterly quota of inductees into the nuclear training pipeline, I likely could have been approved for the one-year postponement I needed to earn a master's degree.

# 2

# OFFICER CANDIDATE SCHOOL

## LEADERSHIP LESSON 2.A.
## FOCUS ON ONE ISSUE AT A TIME.

The jubilation of graduating from college was short lived. The family gatherings and congratulatory words were nice, but all too quickly I would be heading to Newport, Rhode Island, for Officer Candidate School (OCS). A few days prior to my reporting date, my recruiter called to share a few pointers: Buy a couple of Master Lock combination padlocks. Don't bother packing civilian clothes, just bring a laundry bag, gym shorts, white T-shirts, sweat socks, running shoes, and a bathrobe. Don't waste money on a haircut, they'll provide a regulation cut on base. None of the suggestions should have been terribly surprising, but I was beginning to wonder if knowing this information during the recruitment phase two years prior would have had any bearing on my signing decision.

I trusted the Navy's travel service to make necessary arrangements to Newport, Rhode Island. They knew where I needed to be and when I needed to be there. Surely, they would deliver me to the proper destination in a timely manner.

The itinerary looked simple enough. I was to fly from Seattle early Sunday morning, suffer a brief layover in Chicago, then catch a turbo-prop jump into Rhode Island where I would catch a Navy shuttle to the base for a leisurely Sunday evening arrival prior to commencement of classes Monday morning.

The flight from Seattle was uneventful, save the turbulent landing in Chicago. I struggled for a few moments at O'Hare International Airport trying to locate the connecting flight. Perhaps it was a case of nerves associated with the trepidation of this entire new journey, but time seemed to slow as I waited in the concourse terminal. The scheduled boarding time came and went, and it was becoming obvious that something was awry. A gate agent announced a mechanical delay with the aircraft and promised that we would shortly be on our way. My fellow passengers and I commiserated. Loudly. As luck would have it, there were two other officer candidates needing to make this same connection, so the three of us banded together for the balance of our journey.

We should have been in Newport and moved in already by the time we finally boarded the cramped aircraft. Hungry, nervous, and exhausted from the stench of spent aviation fuel fumes circulating about the cabin, we belatedly taxied for our launch to Rhode Island. The night was stormy and the ride was unpleasant as the noisy aircraft pitched and lurched through the wet, turbulent sky. By the time we finally landed, many of the passengers had located their "comfort" bags (read: barf bags) in the seat back in front of them.

It was well past midnight when the other intrepid officer candidates and I rejoined with terra firma, but now we faced a new dilemma. The Navy shuttle that was to take us from the airport to the base was no longer running. With only moderate effort, we were able to summon a taxicab. The real challenge would be in identifying our desired final destination. The cabbie knew of several bases in the area, and he needed to know not only which base to go to, but to which gate at that base and then to which building. Assuming we could get to the right base and gate, he hoped we would be able to determine directions to the actual building that was our ultimate destination. Funny thing about our printed duty orders was that they clearly identified the date, time, and name of the command where we were to report for duty, but they were painfully vague when it came to an actual street address.

After burning through all the cash we had between the three of us to pay for cab fare and touring what felt like the entire greater New England region, we somehow found ourselves at the hallowed halls of Officer Candidate School in Newport around four a.m. The night-shift guards split our trio between three separate OCS companies and sent us to different floors and wings of the building to join our respective outfits. After the uniformed guard showed me to my shared room, which he called a "hole," he instructed me to make my "rack" in the dark without waking my slumbering roommate and to get some shuteye before reveille came at 0530. I fumbled my way through unfolding a sheet and bedspread over the bare mattress before collapsing in utter exhaustion.

## LEADERSHIP LESSON 2.B.
## ESTABLISH AN APPROPRIATE VETTING PROCESS.

I had just entered a deep sleep when all hell broke loose. In my groggy state, I saw an animated man leaning over me, pounding on the wall over my head and screaming some incomprehensible information to someone next door. Disoriented and startled, I swung defensively at the intruder and objected, "Stop it! What's going on?"

"WAKE UP! Get up and fall out on the line in five minutes or the company will do extra time on the grinder!" What language was this? I was slowly coming to realize that the intruder who delivered my rude awakening was my new roommate. "Hurry up!" he continued to shout while donning a robe and frantically making his bed. Head clearing and now understanding that he meant me no harm, I followed his lead, putting on the bathrobe the recruiter had advised that I bring and standing in the hallway outside the door to one side of my hole with my yet-to-be-introduced roommate on the other.

This, seemingly, was reveille, and the first day of Hell Week. Still totally disoriented and bewildered, I was ordered to get my rack presentation-ready and to fall out for head call. While I remade my bed, er, rack, my roommate waited for the guard to walk away before whispering his name while extending a hand in introduction. "Jesse James Lockhart. I'll show you how to make your rack later. Just try to get the wrinkles not to show for now. Welcome to OCS."

Khaki-clad sentries marched us single file to the dormitory-style head (restroom), where we were told when to use the toilet, when to brush our teeth and shave, and when to shower. Three minutes were allotted at each station. Three minutes to shower; three minutes to towel off, comb hair, and shave; three minutes to brush teeth and floss; three minutes in a stall to defecate, should your bowels be trained to perform on command (or, more likely, to hold it until a later opportunity). After such an impossibly short time at each station to complete the necessary task, we marched in our ordered file back to our holes to change from bathrobes into the uniform of the day. For most who had arrived on time, this was no problem since they already possessed the prescribed khaki uniform. I did the only thing that I could and put on my rumpled, dank civilian street clothes from the prior day's travel ordeal, an offense that earned me an isolated trip to the company officer downstairs.

I had naively expected some sort of appreciation for the fact that I had arrived only two hours earlier. Another uniformed guard who walked with strict intent, squaring corners and rapping his heels together at each stop, led the way to the company office. My mind, though foggy from the lack of sleep, was racing as I attempted to decipher what action on my part would make this crazed lunatic stop shouting at me. "ATTENTION!"

He had my full attention. What more could he want? "CAJORIZE!" As I searched frantically about for any sign as to what I should be doing differently, the orders only escalated. If I moved, he shouted. If I attempted to speak, even to ask what he wanted me to do, he shouted. If I looked about for a clue as to what he expected of me, he shouted more loudly. If I stood still, he shouted. Perhaps his vocal cords needed a rest; the verbal abuse subsided for a few moments while I completed some obligatory paperwork. A kind lady who handled the forms quietly offered that when I came to attention I should stand more rigidly, arms locked straight at my sides, and heels locked together with feet oriented apart 45 degrees. Who knew? Her compassion proved she was not part of the game. Her tips helped me to make the bouts of "ATTENTION!" subside, but I clearly offended the guards still by not knowing how to respond to "CAJORIZE!"

Misery loving company, it turned out that several of us across all companies of OCS lacked acceptable attire, so the next order of the day for us laggards was a guided march across base to the uniform shop. I had never before experienced the muggy New England summer weather. The blazing sun that followed the previous night's rain made for a palpable humidity heavier than the best wet sauna. By the time we reached the uniform shop, we were drenched forehead to toe in streams of sweat. Once inside, we marched through a production line where we accumulated khaki slacks, khaki shirts, khaki hats, khaki web belt, brass belt buckle, black socks, black shoes, little brass insignia, and a chintzy sewing kit. Beyond waist size and shoe size, no one asked what we wanted; they simply tossed items into our arms as we proceeded along the defined line. After signing a tab committing to pay for our new uniforms, we marched back to our holes where we were given roughly half the time that could reasonably be expected to change into our uniforms and to stow the balance of our new wardrobes before the guards rushed us out to rejoin our respective companies.

Bedecked in our fresh-from-the-bag, unhemmed, rumpled uniforms, we marched outside to join our companies on the drill field. We marched straight, we marched left, we marched right. Within minutes, it was clear that the combination of brutal heat, humidity, and brand-new black leather shoes would do serious bodily damage; my feet were not going to last. The rigid shoes felt like rough-cut sabots with sharp edges; in the blazing sun they were ill-fitted ovens on my feet, and the blisters were growing fast. The torture would last until we got the entire company marching synchronized as a unit. We needed to march in a smooth unison and, given the unlikely collection of civilians in the group, it was going to take awhile. We marched in circles on "the grinder" until the khaki green of our uniforms gave way to an angry, skin-clinging brown from the perspiration that saturated every fiber.

The march to the barber shop was welcome by now. There was no air conditioning, but the shop was in the basement, and with the fans blowing, the perspiration-wet uniform evaporation-cooled nicely. My time in the barber's chair lasted mere seconds. The electric clippers pressed uncomfortably into the sides and back of my head, but the regulation cut was not all bad. The close buzz was much cooler in this summer heat than the mop I had worn in and there was certainly no one here I would be trying to impress with my nappy locks. And as an added bonus, the cut required zero hair care and would shave precious minutes from my timed morning prep routine. Though I would not have the luxury of sleeping in a few more minutes past reveille, at least now I would be less harried as I showered and groomed during the allotted head time. With no hair to speak of, a quick rinse in the shower and towel dry on my way out would suffice; there can be no bad-hair day when there is no hair to be out of place.

The orientation classes might more appropriately have been named the "disorientation" classes to better set expectations. Everyone was physically drained, many were also emotionally depleted, and our sleep-deprived brains were not in any condition to retain new information. Heads were bobbing as the lectures wore on, and it seemed an eternity before we marched off to the mess hall. Then it was back for "field day," which meant performing janitorial services in the building we occupied, before we were finally retired to our holes for the night. It was past 2000, or eight o'clock at night—surely now we could sleep after fifteen hours of constant activity, right?

Not this week. I was lucky to have been assigned Jesse James Lockhart as my roommate. Jesse had been the animated man pounding on the wall over my head for the morning's rude awakening. He had experienced our next-door neighbor's tendency to sleep too soundly and be slow to fall out for the morning parade to the head. Rather than have the entire company march on the grinder to atone the sins of the one heavy and late sleeper, Jesse had taken up the practice of pounding on the wall and shouting to roust the company slumberer.

Jesse had time in service as an enlisted petty officer and had arrived on base the week prior for a pre-OCS indoctrination. He understood what we were experiencing and knew how to play the OCS game. Jesse explained that this week of hell was to simulate the life of a POW. He explained that whispering through the electrical outlets was the surest means of communication between rooms/cells/holes. This entire Hell Week was to be one marathon test, both of physical limits and of mental will. They would do their best to break us, to get us to quit. Our task was to persevere. The week would culminate in "The Maze," a test of mental retention and ability to follow precise instructions. By the end of the week everyone would know who was capable of withstanding the regimented environment and integrating into a team, and who would head back to whatever life they had before their quick stay at the Hotel OCS. No, there would be no sleep, no rest for us during these 168 hours.

Our job now was to quietly await lights out, then to sneak out of bed, cover the door cracks with towels or other available material to prevent any stray light from leaking into the hallway to be detected by the guards, then turn on dim reading lamps to study the material we had accumulated during the day's orientation classes. That was all Jesse had planned to do before tomorrow's reveille. For me, however, now was the time to hem the issued khaki trousers, to properly fit name tags, company colors, and those little brass insignia to my uniforms. I had to properly prepare my uniform before reveille or there would be hell to pay at the morning inspection. Recalling the manner in which this first day began, I now appreciated the need for the chintzy sewing kit. I also suddenly appreciated that the public school system had forced me to endure Home Economics in the eighth grade, where I learned how to hand stitch a button and do basic clothing repairs. The hems made that night by hand in near darkness were not pretty, but they would do.

There was no improving the shoes, however, and the injuries they caused were debilitating. Those black leather shoes had looked innocent in the cardboard box, but the blisters they first created, then cut, before continuing to gouge away flesh from heel, ankle and toe, left several of us in Juliett company with blood-soaked socks and raw wounds to be aggravated further each day. The white crystals that appeared each night around the creases in the leather shoe top would make for a failed inspection. The source of the mysterious crystals was not fully understood until weeks later—it was the salt residue left after drying our sweat-drenched shoes.

The Maze to end indoctrination week tested both our ability to retain knowledge and to follow orders in a sleep-deprived state. During the marches on the grinder, we had learned to take precise 30-inch steps and to turn crisply 90 degrees left or right as ordered. For this final test, the entire floor of an indoor gymnasium had been configured as a sort of invisible labyrinth. Lacking walls, paths, or guideposts of any kind, The Maze consisted of our senior classmen from across all companies at OCS positioned precisely at specific points on the wooden floor. We "indocs," the zombies running on adrenaline after a true week of hell, were each marched to an individual starting point where a senior classman would ask a question such as, "Who is the CNO?" Knowing not just that the CNO is the chief of naval operations, the professional head of the United States Navy, but also being able to name the person currently holding that position, would earn a set of marching orders, for example, "Turn left 12 paces. Turn left 7 paces. Turn right 8 paces." Each set of precise instructions given in exchange for a correct answer would bring me to the next station. If each turn was a crisp 90 degrees and each step exactly 30 inches, I would arrive at the correct station where another question and set of marching orders awaited. Indocs were marching helter-skelter between stations, crossing paths, avoiding collisions and trying not to lose step count while trying to remember Navy trivia. A wrong answer or arriving somewhere other than the proper station would earn a restart to The Maze. Going astray a second time would earn expulsion from OCS.

Fully stressed, concentrating to hear my next challenge question above the din of other indocs currently marching, listening to, or answering their own set of questions, the senior classman standing before me at the latest challenge station asked, "Who is the captain of the *Enterprise*?" Taking this all quite seriously, I racked my depleted brain for an answer. The USS *Enterprise* is a nuclear-powered aircraft carrier. I had learned the names of many other officers and dignitaries over the past 168 hours, but I must have missed this one. I scrolled through the dozens of names in my head and after a pause that surely was too long for this situation, I resorted in defeat to the only answer learned during the week that came to mind: "I do not know, but I will find out, sir." His eyes grew wide as he said in disbelief, "You don't know that James T. Kirk is the captain of the Starship *Enterprise*?" It was several seconds after he burst into laughter that my mind comprehended the *Star Trek* joke. He had not said "USS" *Enterprise*. I had assumed that. Unknown to me, I had passed The Maze and this was his idea of a happy joke to celebrate my success. Very funny. I have always taken pride in having a good sense of humor, but to this day, I have never laughed at that joke.

By the end of Hell Week, several of our company had washed out and I had snatched nearly eight hours of sleep in total. Had the shuteye been contiguous, it may have been refreshing. But at least the most problematic of our compatriots were gone. Serving group punishment each time one of the non–team players failed to follow orders or was simply incapable of complying had gotten old the first day. Those departed would not be missed. Those of us who survived Hell Week and The Maze could now settle into the OCS routine as rightful members of our assigned companies rather than as newbie indocs.

Morning came early with a zero-dark-thirty run around the base. What better way to embrace the day than to rise before the sun and jog a couple of miles with my classmates? With time and social interaction both precious commodities, we quickly learned to jog at a pace that covered the required ground in the allotted time while allowing at least halting speech between inhales so that we could quiz one another on the impending day's coursework. Next came a brief trip to the head for a miserly shower and shave, then a moment at our holes to don the uniform of the day. Fully assembled as a company, we would march to the chow hall to gulp down breakfast before falling back into formation for the march to class. Between classes, we marched with squared corners to the next assigned classroom. A morning full of classes gave way to lunch, which we attended in the same manner and consumed in the same quick-time fashion as breakfast. Afternoons generally repeated the morning's sequence of events, except for the days with scheduled PT. Dinner was taken in the same urgent manner as breakfast and lunch, and in the evenings, there would be field day activity to clean each space to inspection standards. To end the day was studying before lights out.

One fine New England morning, it was my turn to serve as officer in charge of the Baby Julies, as our senior classmen affectionately referred to the underclassmen of Juliett company. We assembled and marched to breakfast chow, marched to the assigned classrooms, and made it to lunchtime, all without incident. As we assembled outside the classroom building for our march back for lunch, the angry purple clouds that had been darkening for the past several hours began to hurl down rain. Within seconds of commencing our march, the rain became an airborne river, with accompanying winds that saturated our cotton khaki uniforms to a deep shade of brown. The white noise of the pounding downpour made it difficult to hear our cadence call Jody (the ditty used during training marches to synchronize everyone's footfalls), and my classmates began to fall out of step. One of the prior enlisted men within our ranks shouted to me that we should double-time it back to the chow hall. Accepting what seemed like a reasonable suggestion under the circumstances, I ordered us to double our march pace into a near jog for the rest of the journey.

Safely indoors from the drenching storm, we appeared to have just swum ashore from a shipwreck. Water streamed from soaked uniforms that clung tightly to our bodies as rivulets gushed from our leather shoes with each step. As we stowed our soaking covers and briefcases in preparation for lunch, a senior classman approached and informed me to immediately report to our company officer.

"You trashed me out!" he shouted as soon as he saw me. "The CO just chewed my butt for the complete lack of military bearing displayed by Juliett company! What were you thinking?" It seems that an officer just happened to be driving on base when he witnessed our imperfect hustle in the rain and felt an obligation to phone the CO's office to report the infraction. I started to defend my thinking that getting my colleagues out of the inclement weather was the primary goal before realizing his question had been rhetorical.

I settled on apologizing for bringing embarrassment to him and Juliett company before glumly making my way back to the chow hall to rejoin the company. I no longer had the appetite nor the time to eat lunch.

Friday mornings had a slightly modified routine that included company personnel inspection. For the uninitiated, a personnel inspection consists of each person in the company doing his or her level best to impersonate a uniform shop mannequin. Don the creased and spit-polished uniform as flawlessly as possible, hope that every last hair and whisker stays in place, and stand motionless while someone of authority moves from person to person, noting even the slightest imperfection in excruciating detail. Jesse explained before our first inspection that I would do well to purchase a special uniform, complete from cover to shoes, to wear only during personnel inspections. Good tip.

During our first personnel inspection standing, the inspecting officer stepped uncomfortably into my personal space to size me up, so close the visors of our covers were nearly touching. I met his gaze and he met me with a shout of "CAJORIZE!" There was that order again, and still I wasn't sure what it meant. Meanwhile, I was earning some serious demerits, judging by the furious scratching on the inspection tally clipboard. Once safely back in our hole to collect our books for class, and to yo-yo out of the inspection uniform and into one suited for daily wear, I finally asked Jesse to decipher that damned "cajorize." He laughed so hard he could barely breathe, nearly causing the further infraction of a late fallout for class as he wiped tears from his eyes. It seems cajorize is an order given by a superior to an unworthy underling to look away—to "cage your eyes." We are meant to look only at the back of the head of the candidate in front of you or directly ahead into the distance if alone or first in line. A subordinate is not to eye a superior. Who knew?

The only other deviations in our weekday routine occurred for medical or dental appointments, or to stand watch. There were various stations to tend and duties to perform around OCS and each officer candidate stood duty as assigned. Those with solid grades generally were assigned duty during class hours or the night shifts. It was during one of my midnight shifts patrolling the halls that I did the mental calculation on pay rate. With the hours I was working, I was earning roughly $1.75 per hour. Toiling in the farmer's fields as a high school student had been more lucrative. There is more to life than money, but I must admit to wondering if I had made an ill-advised career decision.

## LEADERSHIP LESSON 2.C.
## PERFORM UNDESIRABLE TASKS.

Two noteworthy exceptions to the predictable OCS routine were command inspection and inoculation days. A command personnel inspection is the mother of all inspections. Whereas the regular company inspections are done by a company officer, the command inspection is personally conducted by the big-boss OCS commanding officer (or CO), and the stakes are considerably elevated. A poor showing on a company inspection reflected poorly on you as an individual; a poor showing at a command inspection would "trash out" not only the unkempt individual but the company officer and fellow officer candidates as well. More than just a challenge in personal presentation, the command inspection was also a test of endurance. The weekly company inspections were performed simultaneously by each company officer, making them a mere wind sprint when compared to the command inspections that could only be performed one company at a time. Standing at parade rest or at attention for hours on end left the lucky individuals with only severe shoulder, knee, back, and neck cramps. The unlucky individuals passed out and performed the most horrid of OCS acts, the "skull deck." During one such session, we were all presented at close quarters inside the sweltering summer gymnasium. The only audible disturbance was the periodic murmur of the commanding officer from across the facility as he noted an imperfection on one of the candidates. There suddenly came a brief rustling sound as someone's knees buckled followed by the hollow reverberating "whock!" of a head meeting the gymnasium floor. My personal trick for enduring the command inspections was to occupy my mind with counting the beads of sweat that formed and itched and tickled down my back until meeting my undershirt and being absorbed where my clasped hands set against my lumbar at parade rest.

Inoculations represented the other deviation in routine. To ensure health and readiness to serve anywhere in the world, the military inoculates all members against every conceivable disease, or so it seemed to us human pincushions collecting the vaccinations. On inoculation days, we would be herded through an assembly line of shots organized in the same gymnasium where The Maze and command inspections occurred. Sleeves rolled and bunched up to our shoulders, we passed through a gauntlet of stations left and right, alternating between a quick swap of alcohol and a stab with the needle into our deltoids. Recruits learned early on that the most valuable document in one's possession, much more important than a college diploma or driver's license, was one's immunization record. The rule was simple: You either proved you had valid immunizations for the shots of the day or you faced the gauntlet.

On one fine fall morning at the end of the immunization line, an obviously nervous young trainee was armed with a pneumatic syringe, a gun that blasts the serum under the skin with the squeeze of the trigger. Her trainer loaded a bottle of serum and test fired it into a trash can—psing! The quantity of moisture soaking the side of the can was impressive. Could that possibly be the proper dose? Being first in line (curse the alphabetical ordering), I was about to find out. Aiming high above her head on my left deltoid, she flinched when pulling the trigger. Something felt wrong, and in the instant it took to turn for a look at my upper arm, the blood had already streaked nearly to my elbow. The glancing blow from the gun served more to rip open my skin than to inject the serum. Eyes wide in horror, the trainee was beyond apologetic and began fumbling for cotton, gauze, and a bandage. The trainer dispassionately commented to her, "That happens sometimes," before turning his gaze to me saying, "You'll need another dose." I guess we all have to learn sometime.

Weekends started with "mandatory fun" at 0600 on Saturday morning. Unlike standard PT during the week, on Saturdays there were intercompany competitions in myriad sporting events from swimming, water polo, and basketball to ultimate Frisbee and foot races. All companies rotated through each of three venues: the field, the gymnasium, and the swimming pool. Every company and every OC had the opportunity to participate in each discipline. Everyone had the chance to volunteer if passionate about a particular event, or would become a "military volunteer" in various events to fill a roster. The company officers ensured participation by all OCs. Events tended to be relays or team competitions, to avoid any encouragement of "I"ndividual behavior. The entire company engaged in each sport, and those not actively competing in the fray cheered to provide moral support from the sidelines.

Cage ball crab soccer was the poster event for Mandatory Fun. The cold, wet grass on a drab gray morning is exactly where no one wants to be, especially not squatted backward, belly-up, with hands supporting body weight while trying to kick a 48-inch ball. Moving about the field in crab-walk fashion, our light-gray OCS sweatshirts and pants quickly became dark gray, cold, and heavy as they accumulated the moisture of the previous night's rain and morning fog from the tall turf grass. Catching a cold, soggy cage ball in the face will awaken anyone faster than the best cup of coffee.

While two companies were engaged in a match of cage ball, two more would be participating in shuttle relays and ultimate Frisbee. The shuttle relay field had orange cones demarcating a rectangle 40 yards deep. In a similar setup to swimming relays, two teammates at a time would take their positions on opposing ends of the field, leadoff and third legs on one end facing their second and anchor-leg teammates on the other. The leadoff runner would sprint full throttle to the 40-yard line where the second-leg runner awaited. As soon as the first runner crossed the line, the second-leg runner would launch off, and so on with the third and anchor runners. The rapid back-and-forth dashes could be good fun to watch when the competition was brisk.

I enjoyed the distinct pleasure of attending OCS at the same time as collegiate champion sprinter Charlie Davis. Mr. Davis, also a Juliett, was in the senior class eight weeks ahead of me. He was the anchor leg on a Juliett shuttle relay in which we were hopelessly behind on the day I first witnessed his gift. The opposing company's fourth man was already 10 yards gone and building momentum toward the race finish when our third man crossed the line for Davis to launch. In a stunning, almost comically impossible burst of speed, he accelerated with such controlled yet explosive strides that he devoured the deficit distance from his starting position and crossed the finish line two full strides ahead of the astonished competitor. Watching Davis accelerate at will to obliterate the best sprinting efforts of mere mortals became a high point to the Mandatory Fun mornings.

Ultimate Frisbee as a game was fun, although not entirely so at 0600. Seven players each from two companies took the open field at a time. The game was like a gentler version of football with no ball-running, only passing of the disc allowed. The team on offense aimed to pass the disc from teammate to teammate to make it into the end zone and score a point, while the defense ran to intercept the disc when possible and otherwise to prevent a catch in the end zone. Fast-paced, great exercise, and team building wrapped into friendly competition.

The "track" forming the perimeter around the field activities was actually pavement and drivable by car. More round-cornered rectangle than oval and half a mile in circumference, it was twice the distance of a standard track. The four tighter corners with four straightaways rather than just two rounded corners connecting two straight stretches took a bit of getting used to, but as a former distance runner, I found the longer straights allowed for faster run times and took to it more readily than those who viewed running with the opinion, "Your sport is my sport's punishment." When competing on the track in high school, I preferred racing the mile or two mile to the half mile. When we needed the points in a track meet and coach put me in the half mile, he would advise, "Just remember it is half as far and twice as fast as the mile." Come time for the OCS mile relay, with two runners passing the baton at the quarter-mile half lap and one runner completing a full lap anchor leg, I "volunteered" for the anchor position. My pace around the half-mile track was yawn inducing compared to the speed of Davis in the shuttle relay, but with sub-2:00 split times, I closed lead gaps and passed a fair share of runners to cinch wins for team Juliett.

Mandatory Fun basketball in the gymnasium was organized chaos. Essentially a street pick-up game between two companies, the pace was frenetic and competition intense. This was the realm of my roommate, Mr. Lockhart, who was a devastating talent in complete command on the court. Lightning quick, agile, and possessing superior ball-handling skill, the man simply had game. His effortless moves, intense concentration on defense, and broad smile on offense as he sunk the ball through the hoop belied a person in his true happy place. I had played some basketball prior to OCS but was content to take in the action from the bench, massively outclassed by the talent on display.

The swimming pool we used for water sports was the same facility in which each OC had to prove a fundamental ability to swim and to pass the survival float test. Saturday morning swim events included the standard strokes: freestyle, butterfly, backstroke, breaststroke, and medley. The intercompany relay race competitions allowed those OCs who swam as if with gills and fins to display their talents. As I did with basketball, I remained a spectator during the competitive swimming events. And when I was required to demonstrate my swimming proficiency, I worked to avoid excess water intake from those true swimmers powering past in the next lane.

## LEADERSHIP LESSON 2.0.
## READ THE CONTRACT.

Most of the OC attrition occurred in the early weeks. A few may have been removed involuntarily for major infractions but most resigned on their own, undone by the unbelievable physical, mental, and emotional stress. The sleep deprivation, the blistered feet, the physical fitness tests, the rapid pace of coursework and interminable exams, the watchstand-ing duties, and new concept of military bearing gave every last person pause to reflect, and it ultimately proved to be more than some could endure. It was one of my reflective low points that I learned the true meaning of that ream of paperwork I had signed two years prior in D.C. For most of the officer candidates, dropping out meant returning to civilian life, or for those already enlisted in the Navy, they would be ordered elsewhere to complete their enlistment. For the NUPOC, however, failure to complete OCS represented a one-way ticket to the fleet for service as an enlisted petty officer. "Nuclear waste" was the epithet assigned to NUPOCs unable to earn a commission. Enlistment in the armed forces is an admirable service to the country, but after four years of study invested in an engineering degree, the prospect of joining the enlisted kids straight from high school added a bit more pressure to the NUPOC's OCS experience.

## LEADERSHIP LESSON 2.E.
## IT TAKES A TEAM TO THRIVE.

The bonds I formed during such stressful conditions were amazing. Up to that point I had tended to befriend others with similar interests or backgrounds to my own. In this environment where reliance upon others was imperative for both team and individual success, we quickly learned who possessed which talents, and the team naturally placed the best resources on each arising challenge. The group dynamic was to ensure our collective success by volunteering those with the most fitting skills for any task, no matter how pleasant or loathsome that task might be. To complete the virtuous circle, as individuals we readily stepped up to accept the challenges where we believed we would prevail. Each of us craved the satisfaction of successfully conquering a challenge, both to satisfy our own individual egos and to prove our worthiness to others, and in so doing to ensure ourselves a position within the team. In this symbiosis between individual and team, lasting bonds quickly formed between individuals who likely would have had nothing to do with one another in free society.

## LEADERSHIP LESSON 2.F.
## ASK STUPID QUESTIONS EARLY.

After eight weeks, we were happy to have made it through the first half of OCS yet sorry to see the senior half of our company graduate into their next assignments. The halfway point was more than a milestone marked by the passage of time. It marked the passing of leadership and tradition from one class to the next. One of the fascinating aspects of OCS is that for all its military discipline and success, there are no formally trained drill instructors. The senior class indoctrinates the junior class, and in just eight short weeks, the cycle repeats itself. Incoming civilians transform from bewildered, plain-clothed men and women to proper bearers of military etiquette to instructors on the military way of life—all in just eight weeks. To be sure, not everyone makes the transition and the weeks are 24/7, not 8/5. But the compassion the seniors have for the juniors from having been there themselves, touched by just a hint of desire for payback, results in a miraculously successful formula.

Military protocol has junior personnel greet their superiors in the chain of command with a salute as a sign of respect. The Navy has a tradition in which a newly commissioned officer recognizes the first enlisted person to salute not only with a returned salute, but also with a silver dollar. On graduation day, the day I received my officer's commission, I was only too happy to hand my traditional silver dollar for my first returned salute to a salty senior chief petty officer who had served as one of our OCS instructors. As I shook his hand and offered sincere thanks for the many pearls of wisdom and naval folklore he had shared with us, he replied, "Always remember, sir, as an ensign you're expected to be stupid. Just don't abuse the privilege."

The letter congratulating me upon selection as a NUPOC understated the transition in describing OCS as "an environment totally different from your civilian lifestyle."

**COMMANDER**
**NAVY RECRUITING COMMAND**

6 JUL 1982

Dear Mr. Barnhart,

    Congratulations on your selection as a nuclear propulsion officer candidate. You have been selected as one of the elite from a truly outstanding group of applicants and can be justifiably proud of your accomplishment. This is a significant step on your way to fulfilling a position of prestige and responsibility in the nuclear Navy.

    When you report to Officer Candidate School (OCS), you will find yourself in an environment totally different from your civilian lifestyle. You will undergo an intense course of instruction designed to provide you the principles of leadership, discipline, teamwork, physical fitness and the basic general knowledge required to be a Naval officer.

    Each part of the training at OCS, the Nuclear Power School and Prototype has a purpose. If a candidate cannot cope with the pressure during the initial training course, he could never cope with the pressure he would encounter in the Navy. You have been selected from your peers because you have established a record of succeeding, and this record identifies you as a person of the caliber required to succeed in the Navy. I am confident you can meet this challenge.

    I welcome you to the Navy team.

Sincerely,

J. D. WILLIAMS
Rear Admiral, U. S. Navy

Mr. James Louis Barnhart

## LEADERSHIP LESSON 2.G.
## NEVER CONFUSE "WILL DO" WITH "CAN DO."

Those who have completed OCS will tell you they know themselves better than they previously imagined possible. They have seriously tested their perceived personal limits, continued well beyond what they believed those limits to be, and in so doing have broadened their self-knowledge and reset their personal life expectations to dramatically higher levels. For better or for worse, many in the world will go their entire lives and on to their graves without knowing their true personal limitations or capabilities. This knowledge is the difference between "will do" and "can do."

## LEADERSHIP LESSONS:

**2.A.** Focus on one issue at a time. It is easy to become overwhelmed when a plan goes awry, fretting about what to do next, wondering why this is happening to you, considering who could possibly help—the thoughts may pass rapid fire through your mind or pile up until it feels like you're facing a mountain. Rather than working yourself into a frenzy of scattered thinking, recognize that everyone experiences inconvenience. Remain calm, focus on the most pressing issue, and move forward with the most logical solution presently available.

**2.B.** Establish an appropriate vetting process. Finding the right recruits is fundamental to the success of any team. Hell Week tested the mettle of new entrants in a manner that filtered out early on those whose character or mental or physical resilience would limit their individual—and the team's—ultimate success. The OCS vetting process would be inappropriate in the civilian sector, but appropriate aptitude assessments, phone screens, interview panels, one-to-one interviews by select team members, or sample presentations by candidates can effectively identify and assess potential newcomers. Giving proper time and care to the selection process can help ensure the time and money invested in the onboarding and training new recruits goes toward those who will most likely succeed in your organization.

**2.C.** Perform undesirable tasks. And do them with zeal. Every job involves certain tasks that most people would prefer not to perform. Accept the less desirable tasks with a similar demeanor as you would the ones you find more pleasant and you will set yourself apart. Accepting and completing challenging tasks will build resilience, character, and a reputation as someone who will pull their weight in a team and succeed despite obstacles.

**2.D.** Read the contract. Pay special attention to the fine print. Therein likely is detail that the other party is hoping you will accept without thinking through the potential future impact. Be sure you understand and will abide by any contract before you sign.

**2.E.** It takes a team to thrive. Acting independently, a single person may survive but will not thrive. There simply are too many demands for time and too few hours in a day for a single individual to do more than survive in this brutally competitive world. Don't be too proud to allow others to showcase their strengths; encourage them to perform to their full potential! Also step up for your team where your skills can bring everyone benefit.

**2.F.** Ask stupid questions early. As a new recruit to any career position, avail yourself of the grace period to ask the "stupid" questions. The inquiry and answer that brings needed knowledge in the innocent early days of a new role can signal ignorance, apathy, or perhaps true stupidity when posed later.

**2.G.** Never confuse "will do" with "can do." Learn your true personal limitations. The human mind and body can endure and accomplish much more than most people ever imagine. Most people settle for "will do," a mindset that is constrained by boundaries of effort willingly put forth. True leaders reset the boundaries from "will do" to "can do" by leveraging a true understanding of their personal limitations and capabilities to accomplish far more than others might think possible.

# PART II

# DETERMINED FOLLOWER

Success takes commitment to a course of action. When we are committed to our journey, the inevitable challenges that we encounter will only deepen our resolve to overcome them. Where the unsure follower might see a challenge as a reason to change course, the determined follower sets about learning how to conquer not only the present challenge but also future ones of a similar form.

The determined follower is a leader-in-learning who observes and collects knowledge from the present leader(s) of the journey. They learn from experiencing both good and bad leadership activities. We strive to emulate those inspired leadership moments, while we make note to avoid those leadership lapses that resulted in undesirable outcomes.

# 3

# STASH ENSIGN DUTY

## LEADERSHIP LESSON 3.A.
## EARN RESPECT.

The US Navy has three main avenues for producing new officers: the Naval Academy, the Naval Reserve Officers Training Corps (NROTC) program through public and private colleges, and Officer Candidate School. The US Naval Academy in Annapolis, Maryland, educates officers for commissioning into the United States Navy and Marine Corps with four years of military orientation. The NROTC program is available at various college campuses and adds a dose of military orientation to students otherwise completing a civilian course of study. Officer Candidate School offers a route to an officer's commission to those who have completed a bachelor's degree prior to pursuing a career in the Navy.

The first and most lowly US Navy officer's rank is an ensign, aka "butter bar," for the single gold bar insignia. No matter the path taken to earn the ensign commission, the newly minted ensigns must complete further training in their designated specialty before receiving orders of any real responsibility. I, of course, was headed for the nuclear training pipeline, but as luck would have it, my assigned specialty coursework would not begin for another four months after my OCS commissioning. Such scheduling delays are typical, and the waiting ensigns are "stashed" in menial roles at various commands pending the start of their specialty training. Think of it as the military equivalent of a college internship in the civilian sector. My stash orders sent me to the naval recruiting station in Seattle.

Upon reporting for duty in Seattle, it became immediately apparent that there was no true need for even a single stash ensign. The able staff of recruiters, both officer and enlisted, had the district's recruiting needs fully covered. Nonetheless, I was the fifth stash ensign reporting to the command. The others had been there for weeks or months, depending on the source and timing of their commission, and had the routine down pat. Those who had been there the longest were entrusted with performing interviews for candidates seeking NROTC opportunities. Others proctored various military aptitude tests to civilian applicants, updated military procedure manuals to the latest revision, filed various paperwork, and worked out at the base gymnasium to pass eight hours each day.

Stash duty was awkward at first. The yeomen, the military version of administrative assistants, were a great bunch of people and really knew how to keep the office running. To have these experienced and squared-away career people calling me "sir" was surreal. At OCS, the only enlisted personnel we ever encountered were the senior chief and master chief petty officer instructors. These were career Navy men and women who had climbed the ranks and learned the Navy way of doing things over decades of service. They were clearly the ones in the know, and, since we were officer candidates who had not yet earned our commissions, they certainly never addressed us as "sir" or "gentlemen." Accepting the sir title took some getting used to, and even after the novelty wore off, it still seemed odd that I should have rank authority to give orders to these seasoned professionals. Soon enough I would realize that many who wear an officer's uniform have no such hesitation in wielding positional power. Indeed, the power associated with the uniform was for some other officers the apparent motivation in seeking a commission.

## LEADERSHIP LESSON 3.B.
## EMBRACE CHANGE.

After a few days of chatting with the recruiters and observing the office operations, I had a basic understanding of the recruiting process. The recruiters would pull or buy mailing lists of the desired target demographic, whether it be high school graduates or dentists, then type up mailing labels for the target-appropriate literature and send a mass mailing via USPS. The same recruiting lists could be manually sorted for "smile and dial" cold calling. The IBM Selectric typewriter was the primary office tool at the time, but one astute lieutenant junior grade had the foresight to purchase a couple of personal computers and database software in the hope of improving office efficiency. Seizing the opportunity to add value, one other ensign and I volunteered to establish a recruiting database on the PCs.

Personal computers (PCs) were just emerging, and the software available was nearly as limited as the computer skills of the average populace at that time. The database program could readily sort by any of the selected fields, but the workable data size was severely limited to what could be stored in a single file on the PC's default disk drive. The mailing lists we were dealing with exceeded that many times over, rendering the purchased software useless for the intended task. It took a few weeks of studying software manuals and testing various code manipulations, but we were successful in coding software to modify the database program to allow us to manage data sets across multiple floppy disks. Our modified program would prompt the user for the appropriate disk as needed, allowing us to sort the list by education, geographic location, and other factors. With the target recipients sorted and identified, we set up a mail merge program and routed the output to a printer. For the first time in the Navy's recruiting program, "personalized" letters could be mass produced, complete with address labels, to reach out to the civilian populace in the efficient pursuit of recruitment quotas.

## LEADERSHIP LESSON 3.C.
## RESPECT THOSE WHO HAVE GONE BEFORE YOU.

The senior officers expressed their admiration and appreciation of the computer software work by giving me plum assignments such as local college and high school visits. I was driving a government-configuration white Chevy Citation with the NRD Seattle (Naval Recruiting District) identifier on the doors but at least I was out of the office. Errands varied from posting recruiting flyers and reply card posters in strategic locations around campuses to taxiing recruits from school to their testing and interviewing sites.

Back in the early '80s, simply showing up on campus decked out in a dress blue uniform could be a test of one's mettle. Walking down the hallway of a local high school to the administrative offices, each step on the polished floor crisply echoing my progress, I reflected upon how only four short years earlier I, too, had been an immature high schooler. The enthusiastic guidance counselors and principal welcomed me, almost in awe of having a military officer in their institution to serve as a role model for the rambunctious teenagers. Even as the occasional elder statesman would hail me to share a story from his own military service or someone's grandmother would offer a word of appreciation, the students offered an endless barrage of juvenile insults inspired by the ring-leading delinquents who wanted to prove to their peers how far above military service they were. Funny thing about those insults was that one was never delivered by a lone individual. Only in peer-pressured packs with an attentive audience would some little coward summon up the courage to disrespect me or my uniform.

Even as they feigned disrespect, they trusted I would pass stoically while displaying the professional military bearing that supported their freedom to cast such insults. I especially appreciated the creative verbal jabs about the shine on my shoes—how the sun's reflection from my toes was blinding, it was like walking with mirrors on my feet, or it must have taken days of spit polishing to apply that ridiculous shine. The cowardly punks aimed their jokes with the intent to humiliate me. Too bad they did not understand the pride I felt in wearing that uniform, a key feature of which was those same black leather shoes that had ravaged my feet back at OCS. Now broken in and always attentively hand-polished, the shoes represented a proud accomplishment for me. In their feeble attempts at ridicule, the wayward teens were unknowingly paying me the highest compliment.

## LEADERSHIP LESSON 3.D.
## THE HUMAN MIND IS READILY PERSUADED.

Interviewing candidates for the various officer programs was the true highlight of stash ensign duty. During the first few interviews, I was nearly as nervous as the candidates. I soon established a rhythm, however, learning what questions to ask and how to interpret the responses, and honed the fine skills of perception and insight. I developed the ability to discern most any candidate's motivations by the end of a 30-minute interview, and to assess the likely fit of that person into the rigors of Navy life. Some would be a good mutual fit—good for the Navy and good for the individual. Some would be a good fit for the Navy but not necessarily so good for the individual. Others would not necessarily bring much to the Navy, but the requisite discipline would certainly benefit the individual. I had the positional power to influence the direction of the candidates' lives with a yea or nay vote for recruitment.

On the occasion of encountering a cock-sure candidate who believed the Navy would be lucky to count him among its ranks, I would visualize him in the team-oriented OCS atmosphere. If I could honestly see him being humbled and carrying his load for the team, I would recommend accession. If I saw him playing the chameleon and modifying his outward behavior just enough to slip by OCS without truly absorbing the lessons, only to become an arrogant menace to future subordinates in the fleet, I would vote against him. If I discerned sufficient brazen arrogance to see an obvious OCS flunkee in the making, I had a decision to make. Would the experience of a week or two at OCS before his ultimate dismissal leave a sufficient dent in this candidate's ego to cause further self-reflection and maybe help to create a better person in society in the long run? If so, I just might put forth a positive recommendation. If, on the other hand, it was clear that this person would just be a total waste of everyone's time and flunk out without receiving any lesson, I would stamp the file no.

The really interesting candidates were those bright, articulate future leaders who had no idea what they wanted to be when they grew up. These were the ones that the lieutenant recruiters perceived to be slam dunks, the easy additions to the quota. When meeting with these candidates, I would quickly assess that they would, indeed, make fine officers and then proceed to share with them my experiences to date in the Navy's service. I provided full descriptions of life at OCS, as well as projected career paths. I readily volunteered information that my recruiters a couple of years prior would not have shared even if I had known to ask those sorts of questions. In short, I tried to ensure that these truly high-potential candidates were as thoroughly equipped as possible to make their own best decision regarding military service. I let these high-potential recruits know that I was putting in a positive recommendation, and I encouraged them to make the right personal decision. Some of them ultimately joined the Navy. Some of them, much to the bewilderment of the lieutenants, decided to withdraw their application after interviewing with me and getting a glimpse into OCS life. The outcome was always for the best.

## LEADERSHIP LESSONS:

**3.A.** Earn respect. Do not attempt to demand respect from others or to rely on positional power in an attempt to control subordinates. Although your organization's hierarchy may grant you legitimate positional authority over others, resist the temptation to "pull rank." It is far better to approach subordinates as equal team members than as somehow inferior to you if you aspire to bring out the full team potential.

**3.B.** Embrace change. Change is inevitable. Embrace it and seek ways to improve the present situation into a better future. You need not be on the so-called "bleeding edge" of every change that comes along, but you will do well to keep an open mind to new trends and potential new solutions that could improve your productivity.

**3.C.** Respect those who have gone before you. Whether you admire their achievements or not, respect those who have tread the path you now walk. Even if you have no desire to follow in their footsteps, you will be amazed at the valuable knowledge to be had by taking the time to collect it from those with experience. The enlisted personnel of NRD Seattle shared many insights with me during casual conversations at the water cooler, from the must-experience attractions near various duty bases to inside knowledge on how to score low-cost overnight stays on military bases during travel within the US. These tips would serve me well in the years ahead.

**3.D.** The human mind is readily persuaded. When faced with a decision, seek the advice of trusted and experienced others, then take the time for introspection before committing to a decision. Chances are good that there is more than one valid perspective on any pending decision. Be especially mindful to consider differing input when the decision pertains to career positions that may be open to you. When deciding your career path, know that you alone own the final call. Likewise, when in a position of power, whether formal or informal, be aware of your persuasive influence and strive to provide an unbiased, balanced perspective to others. When speaking with recruit candidates, I could accentuate the personal benefits from attending OCS or just as easily emphasize the myriad challenges to be faced.

# 4

# NUCLEAR POWER SCHOOL

## LEADERSHIP LESSON 4.A.
## TEAMWORK WINS.

The reason for stash ensign duty was to buffer the Navy's training pipeline logistics; junior officers (JOs) could perform menial tasks while awaiting commencement of their assigned Nuclear Power School class. Upon arriving in Orlando, Florida, I immediately appreciated the warm weather even in February. It was snowing in Seattle when I departed, and many of the highways I had driven across the country were treacherous with blowing snow and icy conditions. The first night in town, my body craved movement after being confined to the car driver's seat for the long cross-country drive. To stretch my legs, I went for a stroll wearing jeans and a T-shirt, enjoying the mid-60s nighttime temperature. Locals were bundled up in thick winter coats similar to the one I had worn the prior week to fend off the blowing snows in Seattle. The Floridians were every bit as amazed by my sleeveless attire as was I by their bulky wraps.

One of the nice things about the staggered start dates for the Navy's training curricula was that you seldom could reach a new training command without either knowing someone who was already there or knowing someone who would soon be arriving. In this case, I knew other junior officers both from OCS and from my stash recruiting assignment in Seattle. One of these kind souls was so generous as to allow me to sleep at his place for the first couple of nights while I searched for an apartment of my own. Staying even for a brief few days in someone else's home, it is hard not to notice when the host is always absent.

During one of the brief moments that our paths actually crossed, I inquired about life at NPS (Nuclear Power School). "Life?" was his quizzical answer. "I'd recommend that you enjoy Orlando while you can. Once your classes start, you can forget about it." I had intentionally arrived one week early in order to find a place to call home for the next six months and to have time to arrange delivery of my worldly possessions prior to commencement of classes. It now sounded as though I might also want to take in the local attractions.

At a nearby fast-food joint the next day, I happened across a few other officers in the lunchtime crowd who were nearing completion of their NPS courses of study. Asked for their summary comments, they, too, suggested that I enjoy my freedom before the start of classes. They assured me that from the very first day, the pace at NPS would be unlike any other training I had ever encountered. I was none too worried about a challenging course load, but it did appear that a consensus was forming that this was no walk in the park.

On the first day of NPS, all members of our incoming class reported to an auditorium for placement exams and a pep talk. Our placement exam scores would be used to assign classroom seating, with those scoring higher seated near the back of the class and those who presumably would require more instructor assistance seated in the front. The pep talk might have been borrowed from the script of an animated cartoon, one that is supposed to strike fear even as it entertains. The presiding officers delivered two main messages. The first was that our performance at NPS would follow us throughout our naval careers. Not only would doing well at NPS enable us to call our own shots on initial duty assignments, to select our own home base and desired class of ship, but our scores could be a deciding factor for future duty assignments and promotions. The second message addressed the intensity of the coursework itself, likening immersion in the NPS curriculum to drinking from a fire hose. Few descriptions have ever proven so apt.

Unlike the typical college or even graduate school setting in which the student signs up for select courses based upon desired class schedules, instructor preference, or other convenience factors, all NPS classes were predetermined. To vastly improve efficiency and accelerate the curriculum pace, the students were sequestered to their assigned seats in their assigned classrooms all day. From 0800 to 1700 (eight a.m. to five p.m.) each day, students sat in their same spots while instructors of the various courses rotated classrooms. Rather than enjoying a leisurely stroll across campus or perhaps a schedule break in a library or on a nicely mowed lawn between classes, there only would be a brief interruption while the departing instructor erased the board and the arriving instructor began to write. The lectures were nonstop. Instructors rotated in and out, delivering a continuous barrage of classroom technical instruction. Even our individually assigned lockers were inside our assigned classrooms. With nearly all of the books and coursework material being classified information, none of the material was allowed off the premises. This, of course, meant all study had to be completed on premises.

One rule of thumb from my college days carried over into these military courses: each hour of classroom instruction required one and a half to two hours of time outside class for studying the material and completing the homework. Just as those who had gone before had warned, NPS was a daunting undertaking. By the end of the first week, it was clear that something would have to give. Sitting in the classroom all day taking notes and recording homework assignments due the next day and then sitting in the same room and seat most of the night to complete the assignments was no way to spend six months.

Misery loves company. The new classmates and I huddled one evening to compare thoughts on how to best survive the NPS workload. One thing that was clear to the vast majority of us was that no one person should attempt to make it through NPS alone. There were one or two hermits who either had such extreme confidence in their own brilliance or such a remarkable aversion to social interaction that they resisted overtures to join a study team and opted to go it alone, but most of us saw the wisdom in forming strategic alliances. Given the amazing intellectual talent assembled at NPS, most study teams of four or five students were able to include chemical, mechanical, and electrical engineers, with an occasional nuclear or aerospace engineer to round out the roster.

With study teams assembled, we were better able to establish a rhythm, albeit a frenetic one. The instructors still rotated through the classrooms and delivered new material and homework assignments at a pace easily four times that of a typical college course. We now had the team safety net to back us up, however. Many of us got into a groove where we were able to take notes on the current lecture even while we worked the homework assignment from the previous one. This was an acquired skill, the epitome of multitasking—knowing how to concentrate superficially on one subject even while immersed in another. The challenge was knowing the limits of one's own attention and balancing against the trusted capabilities of study-group teammates. If you believed a fellow student would be able to fill in any blanks in your understanding, you could continue to feverishly work homework problems during the current class lecture. If the questions in your mind seemed likely to exceed what other students could fill in, you had better leave the homework for later and focus singularly on the current lecture. If the lecture content seemed too cloudy or your mind needed a reset, it was time to get a hand in the air for a clarifying question.

Even if you were keeping pace well with the current lecture, it was possible that the prior class's homework was sufficiently involved that the time to complete it was going to exceed the current lecture's allotted slot.

In this case, a prudent clarifying question, while unneeded for the sake of learning, would slow the pace of the lecture just enough to balance with the rate of in-class homework completion. In this intense, multitasking fashion, it was possible to end the class day of instruction with only an hour or so of remaining homework for the evening.

Learning to rely upon fellow students in a synergistic manner was a vital component of the NPS experience. After nearly every lecture, there was someone to be found in the class who had previously studied similar material during their undergraduate work and who could help clear any lingering mental fog. The benefit to those of us acquiring the new knowledge was obvious, but equally important was the benefit to the student imparting knowledge to his or her classmates. The confidence boost from being the one to help enlighten other remarkably intelligent engineers would be just the internal pick-me-up needed to persevere when it could fairly be said that all of us felt like we were struggling in one subject or another.

## LEADERSHIP LESSON 4.B.
## MANAGE TIME.

Another obstacle to overcome at NPS was the exam schedule. A benefit of having the curriculum centrally controlled is that the typical college challenge of having two or three professors decide that next Wednesday would be the perfect day for a midterm exam was never a problem. NPS exams, with the accelerated pace and rotating classes, were scheduled one per week. As painful as it was in college to periodically binge study for an occasional barrage of midterm or final exams, at least the pace allowed for a period of mental and physical rest once exam season had passed. At NPS, there was always an exam looming. Studying for and taking the exams was work enough, but the logistical kinks it put into the multitasking strategy of completing homework in lectures were truly confounding. The usual result was a late night of studying prior to exam day, followed by an extended night the day of the exam to make up the homework that otherwise might have been completed during the lecture period foregone for the exam. Of course, given the weekly workload, most weekends saw students on base studying away the available hours.

## LEADERSHIP LESSON 4.C.
## WEAR COMFORTABLE CLOTHING.

As is the case with every military command, NPS also held periodic personnel inspections. While I cannot recall any inspection ever being a pleasant undertaking, those at NPS were unusually heinous. The official uniform for spring in Orlando, Florida, was the khaki certified navy twill, or CNT. Brilliant military minds being what they are, the CNT uniform had another common name, one that the sharp reader has likely already surmised. CNT is 100 percent polyester woven with thick, nappy ridges like those on a tight corduroy. While this material held a fine crease and looked as sharp as any other 100 percent polyester fabric, CNT had the equivalent thickness of a triple-layer trash bag and was equally unbreathable in the blazing summer sun. As pleasant as was the Orlando weather in February, it had grown stiflingly muggy by June. The truly impressive thunderstorms, replete with blinding lightning bolts and ear-shattering thunder, would dump torrents of rain before giving way to the relentless sun. With humidity nearing 100 percent, we would assemble outside in the equally visible and palpable waves of evaporation to stand inspection.

Any Orlando resident will tell you that it is not possible to towel off and become physically dry after swimming, showering, or bathing. A nice cool shower may leave you feeling momentarily refreshed, but try as you might, you will never be able to towel yourself off to satisfaction. The humidity levels are simply too high, even higher than the ambient temperature; the climate is too frequently at the dew point.

Trying to reach a dry state during spring in Orlando is a frustration similar to what the painter covering the San Francisco Golden Gate Bridge must feel—upon reaching one end, it is time to begin painting anew at the opposite end. The task is simply impossible and sees no end. By the time you towel off one area, the last area visited is condensing and perspiring anew. The locals know to go outside and start the car air conditioner before stepping into the shower. Only by showering, quickly dressing in light cottons, and expeditiously jumping into a pre-cooled and dehumidified vehicle can you hope to make it to the inside of an air-conditioned office for a day in relatively dry comfort. Standing outdoors for inspection in the sweltering heat and withering humidity, we would have rivulets of perspiration running from our temples, arms, and legs during personnel inspections. Through it all, the CNT uniforms held the same appearance as they had coming straight from the cleaner's bag, crisp and plastic.

The mantra throughout NPS was "2.5 to stay alive," meaning that academic performance below a 2.5 grade average on a 4.0 scale would earn the student dismissal from the program. Officers pass through many effective filters to make it to NPS, generally indicating a solid chance for success, and those whose scores suggested academic difficulty received extra attention from the instructors. Even with the many safeguards, not every NPS student was up to the challenge.

The last hurdle at NPS was the comprehensive final examination. It wasn't enough to drink from the fire hydrant for six months, or pass the battery of midterm exams, or successfully complete every individual course final examination. All this was insufficient to prove readiness to continue along the nuclear training pipeline. Each student would also face a comprehensive final examination in which content from any course in the entire NPS curriculum—the equivalent of a two-year master's degree course of study condensed into six intense months—was fair game. The comprehensive exam, a "final final," assessed total retention and would serve as the ultimate metric in an individual's NPS class standing.

## LEADERSHIP LESSONS:

**4.A.** Teamwork wins. Working as a team benefits both the individual and the collective. Collaborating with others enables output many times that which the same individuals could deliver in aggregate when working alone. In short, the whole is bigger than the sum of its parts. Don't choose to go it alone.

**4.B.** Manage time. Time is a precious resource that must be budgeted and spent with care. Write out what goals you intend to achieve and by when. Review your written goals on a regular basis and hold yourself accountable to make steady progress toward your goals in the allotted time. Effective time management is a learned necessity.

**4.C.** Wear comfortable clothing. Don't try to make yourself seem some-one you're not by wearing uncomfortable clothing. Full polyester clothing may retain its appearance over a long day's use, but life is too short to wear something uncomfortable just for appearances. More seriously, what you wear should never make you uncomfortable, whether it be the material, the colors, or the pattern. Your clothing will rarely be what others will remember about you as a leader. In the military, the choice of clothing is made simple by the mandated uniforms. In the civilian sector, use your freedom of choice to dress in comfortable attire that is appropriate to your situation and that conveys a professional image. There are many important matters that will occupy your mind throughout any given day; your choice of clothing should not be a distraction.

# 5

# NUCLEAR REACTOR
# PROTOTYPE TRAINING

The second half of the nuclear training pipeline involved actual hands-on performance in a nuclear reactor prototype facility. This is where classroom theory learned at NPS met actual practice at one of the Navy's highly secure nuclear reactor facilities. By design, the facilities are inaccessibly located on strategically isolated sites. In my case, the site was located somewhere in Idaho, miles from any centers of population.

It was late summer when my incoming class descended upon the Idaho Falls–Blackfoot region. The weather was hot but arid, dry, and dusty, in stark contrast to the humidity of Orlando. The small-town atmosphere was pleasant and the locals cordial, which was important since there was no military base in the area and the steady stream of Navy personnel rotating through their training assignments ensured that temporary housing was limited. There were few apartment complexes, and any desirable vacancies were filled even before they could be listed. Seizing the opportunity to profit from the Navy's presence, many area homeowners would rent rooms or basements in their houses to the migratory students. My fellow officer roommate and I shared the main floor of a small house in which the basement was rented to a young married couple. The back porch where the washer and dryer were located represented the only communal portion of this "duplex," so the situation was perfect. With the marathon shifts that we would be working, our section of the house would rarely be occupied. The town and neighborhood were certainly nice enough, but having a stay-at-home mother living on the same property provided an added deterrent against any vagrant shenanigans.

The Navy boasts the world's finest nuclear reactor safety record. This success has been earned through careful planning and meticulous execution. In practical terms, this meant that our temporary new home would see even less of us. One of the planned safety features of the prototype training site was its physical distance from any population. This remote location provided two obvious benefits to the military and civilian populations. First, any potential risk from terrorist attack was minimized since anyone approaching the site could be seen miles in advance, and the only connecting road was guarded with tightly controlled checkpoints. Only those with proper authorization could pass the armed guards and thorough vehicle searches to access the facility. The second benefit was the minimization of risk to the civilian population should anything ever go wrong at the facility itself. The tremendous distance from civilization ensured that any possible nuclear release, however improbable in the first place, would pose no immediate threat to any civilian or community.

## LEADERSHIP LESSON 5.A.
## FOREGO ENTERTAINMENT TELEVISION AND VIDEOS.

In keeping with the extraordinary security of the facility, personal vehicles of students were prohibited from entering the site. Instead, the Navy provided transportation in the form of school buses contracted for the sole purpose of ferrying students to and from the facility. An added benefit of our shared housing arrangement was its location. Our house was situated just a few doors away from the first bus stop. The advantage of being the first on the bus was that we could select from a ready supply of open seats when heading to work or training. The bad news was that the ride was a 90-minute affair on a good day, and the other stops along the bus route added another 20 minutes to the trip. As we would also discover come winter in Idaho, the buses take quite some time to warm from a cold start, seeming to rely upon passenger body heat as the prime thermal source. The bus interior on an early winter morning evoked childhood memories of a public walk-in freezer, with bitterly cold metal and breath vapor hanging in the air, except the bus offered the added treat of frigid vinyl for seats.

The time-disciplined structure of the prototype facility had us working a twelve-hour rotating shift. Each week the shift worked by any given team would rotate, roughly from days to evenings to graveyard in a never-ending cycle of circadian rhythm disruption. Working twelve hours each day over a prolonged period will wear most people down. Imagine you are scheduled to work from 0800 to 2000 hours (eight a.m. to eight p.m.) for a given week. Now add preparation time to rise, shower, shave, eat breakfast, get dressed, and walk to the bus stop. Also assume that it will be an uneventful bus ride of only 90 minutes. You are now waking by 0545, if you are a quick eater and a fast walker. After twelve hours of work, it is time for the return bus trip home. No need to account for bus loading and unloading times since the transfers are fairly orderly. Feeling hungry by the time you arrive back home? Go ahead and make a quick bite for dinner, but recognize that it is past ten o'clock in the evening by the time you actually walk through your front door. Who can sleep on a full stomach? After a few days on this cycle, you might not care about the full stomach and forego the newspaper and evening news for a few more minutes of bedrest, since 0530 comes around awful early and the day-flipping calendar treadmill will run the same cycle again tomorrow.

## LEADERSHIP LESSON 5.B.
## SLEEP IS OPTIONAL.

Each week, just about the time that your sleep-deprived body has adjusted to the new schedule, the working shift rotates with no more than one day to transition into the next sleep-wake schedule. The transition days are the worst of the bunch; some of the members will sleep, others will strain themselves to stay awake in an effort to force their bodies into the new work hours. Most experiment with a different routine each week and realize there simply is no good way to handle these sleep-wake period transitions.

Recognizing the physical drain this routine places on the students, available at no monetary cost on the premises of the prototype facility was a first-come, first-served bunk room. No frills, just a barracks of bunks with woolen blankets whose bristles would put any off-brand steel wool scouring pad to shame. Bunking on site could easily provide a bonus four hours of rack time (sleep) just by removing the bus transit time to work, and the on-site mess facility (cafeteria) was reasonably priced with food comparable to most small-town diners. The real cost, of course, was that a stayover would need to be planned in advance, including a change of uniform and toiletries, not to mention the need to forego any access to the evening news or mail. The sufficiently exhausted sleeper might not even notice the sagging bunk springs and mattress until the next morning, when painful body kinks and muscle cramps would kick in and linger throughout the following day.

Living under the reactor plant's imposed schedule, my roommate and I never missed a rent payment, and our landlord considered us the ideal tenants. Unfortunately, our observant US postal carrier noticed that no one ever seemed to be home, we never had outgoing mail, and the mail he delivered would sometimes accumulate for a few days in our mailbox before disappearing. In a misguided effort to help, the postman concluded that we must have moved and forgotten to leave a forwarding address, so he took it upon himself to suspend delivery and to return all of our mail to the sender! As busy as we were, it took several days for us to realize that the lack of incoming mail was no coincidence but an intentional act. A few telephone calls to concerned family and friends allayed their fears and allowed us to piece together the puzzle of what was happening to our mail. Credit card issuers were less understanding of the situation, however, and froze accounts, added delinquency fees to bills that had never been delivered, and otherwise forced us to spend our precious time off placing calls and writing letters to reinstate our personal credit.

## LEADERSHIP LESSON 5.C.
## PRACTICE EMPATHY TOWARD OTHERS.

On one bitterly cold winter morning following an overnight stay at the prototype facility, I buttoned my peacoat and leaned into the wind, hoar frost, and gravel crunching underfoot as I made my way from the barracks to the café for a bite of breakfast. Energy stores renewed and body temperature recovering from the quick refill stop, I departed the café's welcome warmth to arrive early at the S1W building, intending to get a jump on the day's studies and systems checkout exams. The sun was just rising and I was walking directly east into the blinding rays as they broke on the horizon, both the sun and the bitter wind causing my eyes to tear. Through my blurred vision, I detected a silhouette forming within the blinding light. Someone was coming toward me, and as the figure drew closer, I began to hear footfalls in the gravel. Switching from squinted attempts at sight to rely instead on my hearing to discern the distance between us, I struggled to identify the person about to pass. To salute a subordinate would be a mild embarrassment; to fail to salute a senior officer would be an infraction of disrespect. A mere stride separated us when I finally caught a glint of gold from his garrison cap, which I surmised to be from the anchor emblem of a chief petty officer. As he passed broadside, I could finally realize the gold oak-leaf cluster of a lieutenant commander and snapped a salute, but my recognition of his superiority came too late for his ego.

The LCDR launched into a firm berating. "You need to show respect, ensign! Do you need refresher training on how to properly salute your superior officer?"

"Sorry, sir. I couldn't see your insignia while blinded by the sun," I replied, stopping and turning to face him. His momentum to the west and mine to the east when we passed one another had reversed our positions relative to the rising sun, with him now facing into the rays and my back now to the sun. As the berating continued, I slowly leaned to the side to allow the sun's full radiance to reach his face. He flinched involuntarily, turning away and raising his hand to block the intense light from eyes. He lost his train of thought and his composure but gained a sudden appreciation for my plight a moment earlier. "I'll let it pass this time," he concluded while hurriedly resuming his westward trek, the sun again at his back.

## LEADERSHIP LESSON 5.D.
## IMMERSION GENERATES UNDERSTANDING.

What the six months of NPS was to theory, the six months of prototype training was to practice. The first weeks were spent in nondescript old classrooms with petty officers instructing us in the hands-on operations of various reactor plant systems. Valve by valve, switch by switch, pump by pump, the petty officers drew out system schematics of all key components and explained the basic operating sequences of the assigned nuclear reactor plant. There were several old plants on site, each an early prototype version of a power plant deployed for maritime service in the fleet. I was assigned to the S1W facility; friends were assigned to A1W. The S and A designators indicate submarine and aircraft carrier, respectively, while the middle number indicates the prototype generation, and the final letter indicates the producer, W for Westinghouse and G for General Electric, for example. My S1W plant was an historic relic. It was the prototype of the power plant used in the first nuclear submarine, the USS *Nautilus*.

The men assigned to work on S1W affectionately dubbed it "Shit, It Works!" And the A1W plant, given its sheer size, many times larger than the S1W facility, was affectionately known as "Alice in Wonderland."

Each system and subsystem of the nuclear reactor plant was a new learning opportunity. We studied every flow of the primary coolant system, for example, including pumps, valves, pipes, gauges, sensors and alarms, and the various acceptable operational configurations, to the point where each student could draw the system schematic and thoroughly explain the function and operation of each component. Every mechanical, electrical, steam, water, and vacuum system in the entire reactor plant system had to be learned to this degree, for both the primary and secondary plants. Only by understanding each individual system could we learn the big picture of the reactor plant's operation. After demonstrating the considerable requisite knowledge via written exams and one-on-one interviews or "checkouts" of each system, we would begin hands-on study of the prototype plant itself, tracing each system hand-over-hand, and locating each of the valves, breakers, gauges, and wires that were now committed to memory.

## LEADERSHIP LESSON 5.E.
## NO ONE PERFORMS TO PERFECTION.

After demonstrating thorough mastery of a given reactor plant system, including the ability to draw the system schematic from memory and to physically locate each of the system components in the plant itself, the student would be eligible to learn actual operation of the system by standing watch under an instructor's supervision. In practical terms, the students would stand watch at each station for a few hours at a time, gaining experience in reactor startup, shutdown, and emergency operational procedures. Each watch period, akin to a work shift in a civilian factory, was riddled with mock disaster scenarios or drills. The instructors, all qualified watchstanders, coordinated each drill in advance and observed or, if necessary, assisted the students in conducting each drill to maintain plant safety. Each drill would then be followed by return of the system to a stable state and critique of the student's performance. By the end of this intense immersion, the student is left with an awesome understanding of every detail of the entire reactor plant and a holistic understanding of system interactions and operations.

One evening while I was standing watch under instruction, a gasket on the feedwater system burst. As the water sprayed and system pressure dropped, I quickly assessed the scenario and called all the theory I'd learned in the classroom into practice to try to immediately correct the situation. The petty officer who was supervising me that evening quickly jumped in and began turning valves and making status reports to the maneuvering room, essentially doing my role for me. Why would he step in? Had I handled the situation wrong?

It wasn't until after we had the plant stabilized and things were calming down that I realized this had not been a drill. The plant had experienced an actual failure. It wasn't he who had corrected my course of action, but I who had performed his role when the actual emergency arose. My rapid assessment of the situation and intended actions were textbook perfect; I had momentarily doubted myself when the petty officer stepped in to take control, thinking that perhaps I was deviating from protocol, but he had simply been executing his responsibility to ensure plant safety. Interesting how perspectives differ: An actual emergency and a mere drill produced the same level of anxiety and action from my under-instruction perspective. To the responsible instructor, a drill is a ho-hum event to observe and critique whereas an actual emergency is an adrenaline-filled time to perform.

Upon successful completion of this prototype phase of nuclear training, the qualified student would be able to accurately predict the expected change in reactor plant parameters due to a given change in a subsystem. For example, if a given valve were to change position from open to closed, the student would be able to accurately explain the expected pressure, temperature, or power changes in other systems of the plant. Applying this total understanding of the reactor plan system in reverse, watchstanders are able to observe their station parameters and, should any indications vary, quickly deduce the likely cause of that variance and ascertain the most appropriate actions to take to stabilize and recover the situation.

After a few months at prototype, the officer students would have demonstrated proficiency on each individual reactor plant system and would either be ready to move into qualification for engineering officer of the watch (EOOW), the equivalent to a factory foreman, or be shuffled aside to a conventional power position elsewhere in the Navy as "nuclear waste," a term of endearment for those who failed out of the nuclear training pipeline. The first watches as EOOW were as intimidating as they were exhilarating. The volumes of data streaming in are extraordinary, and the EOOW must assess, prioritize, and act upon the unrelenting stream without hesitation. It is hard to imagine a role anywhere else that demands such incredible capabilities for multitasking. As the posted quotes around the facility proclaimed, "The key to reactor operational success is an alert, well-trained operator." Each of the supporting watchstanders is not only well-trained in their own area but is also in possession of a firm understanding of the other systems' purposes. Should the EOOW ever display hesitation at the barrage of incoming data, the individual system watchstanders can serve as a ready source of knowledgeable recommendations. The "well-trained" part of the operators' description is unassailable; the "alert" aspect is the subject of more than a few cynical comments from the sleep-deprived, bleary-eyed students during their prototype stay.

The nuclear reactor prototype training culminates with two final examinations. The Final Evaluation Watch, or FEW, physically takes place hands-on inside the prototype control box in the EOOW position. As the plant is put through its paces, the total command of the action and watchstanding ability of the EOOW is judged by a senior qualified officer.

I was as nervous as one would expect the morning of my scheduled EOOW FEW. The watchstander I relieved was a chief petty officer from whom I had learned volumes over the prior months. As I completed my pre-watch preparations and said those magic words, "I relieve you," he responded first with the expected, "I stand relieved," before quickly and quietly adding, "Good luck, sir." Moments after he departed, a request arrived for me to approve the lockout, tag-out (LOTO) of a subsystem for maintenance. The senior officer evaluating my performance studied me intensely as I reviewed the requested LOTO package and considered reactor plant conditions. From the LOTO log, I noticed that a prior LO, still in effect, had contained an error. I voiced the error, and my evaluator asked what I intended to do about it. With some reluctance, I phoned the chief whom I had just relieved and requested his return to correct the LO error that he had approved. There were no further issues during that watch, and I collected the needed FEW completion signature.

Successful completion of the FEW is required to confront the final hurdle, a formal oral review board in which senior qualified members openly assess the total knowledge and comprehension of the student under evaluation. Intended to be intimidating, the review board queries every aspect of the six-month prototype training experience. Meanwhile, the student stands at the white board, explaining each mark as he writes in response to the questions posed. Every last plant schematic, every chemical and nuclear reaction equation is fair game. A single failure in either test is allowed, and between the FEW and final review board, each student is allowed three opportunities to pass. In other words, failing either examination twice, or the oral board once if the student took two tries to pass the FEW, earns a ticket out of the program as "nuclear waste."

## LEADERSHIP LESSONS:

**5.A.** Forego entertainment television and videos. When time is tight, don't waste any of it on entertainment TV or video streaming. You can easily find thought-provoking educational programs to view when time allows. The popular programming viewed by the majority of people, however, is unnecessary. After six months without television or streaming, I found even entertainment shows that had been personal favorites had become too annoying to endure. Try leaving the set switched off for even a week and opt instead for a nice read, a family conversation, or some sort of physical activity during the time you would have devoted to television. You will appreciate what a difference it makes.

**5.B.** Sleep is optional. While this lesson ought not be taken literally—the human body clearly requires sleep on a regular basis—over a multimonth period we conditioned our bodies to require no more than five hours of sleep a day and routinely functioned quite well through waking periods exceeding thirty-six hours. But be certain that a given project or program is both urgent and of utmost importance before putting your mind and body through a prolonged period of sleep deprivation. Such episodes should be the exception, and you should view them as a needed sprint of relatively short duration to complete the project rather than a marathon that becomes "normal."

**5.C.** Practice empathy toward others. It is all too easy to assume the worst in others when they fail to perform as we desire. Rather than assume some nefarious reason for their behavior, take the time to understand the situation from their perspective. The LCDR that morning jumped to the conclusion that I intended to disrespect him and immediately moved to reprimand me without any consideration of the circumstances. With a single step and a slight lean to the side, I allowed him, quite literally, to see things from my perspective, and indeed it changed his view.

**5.D.** Immersion generates understanding. As linguistic experts have known for years, total immersion in a subject matter leads to more than mere rote memorization but actual subconscious processing of the newly acquired material. When entering a new role or encountering new surroundings, dive in with passion and your knowledge will grow in bounds.

**5.E.** No one performs to perfection. Even the chief petty officer I followed in my FEW, who had decades of experience and from whom I and literally hundreds of others had learned volumes, had erred. Finding an error from him had been unexpected, and correcting his error during a graded performance evaluation was uncomfortable. Nonetheless, every one of us will err from time to time, and we must be humble in giving and receiving feedback on errors and correcting those mistakes.

# 6

# SUB(MARINE) SCHOOL

The reward for successful completion of the nuclear power training pipeline was four months of Submarine Officer Basic Course (SOBC, pronounced SO-bik) in Groton, Connecticut. Many chose surface ship duty, but I opted for the more demanding "predator" duty than the more leisurely life of a "target." (An intra-Navy taunt. A submarine moves through deep waters like a predator, while submariners affectionately refer to a surface ship as a "skimmer" or "target." Life aboard a skimmer is decidedly more relaxed; the surface ship maneuvers in two directions while the sub navigates in a 3D environment, for example.)

The exhausted young officers, their minds crammed to overflowing from the intense immersion of the prior twelve months, descended upon Groton in a sort of delirious reunion. Though a mere six months had passed since the Nuclear Power School class had dispersed for the nuclear prototype training period, it seemed we had been gone for much longer. Indeed, from a working hours perspective, prototype training spanned the equivalent of roughly fifteen months and there was much catching up to do, comparing notes on who had washed out, the circumstances of their career demise, and general story-swapping on the epic prototype experience.

SOBC promised to be a veritable vacation compared to the nuclear reactor prototype training we had just endured. Class days were scheduled Monday to Friday, 0800 to 1700, and there were no watches to stand as students. Faced with a mere 40-hour workweek, we joked that we would be working half days. Further adding to the vacation atmosphere was the promise of relatively simple coursework. The subject matter was to be basic submarine systems and construction, with a smattering of basic seamanship. Learning about a few shipboard tanks and communication systems seemed absurdly simple after the complex nuclear systems we had just mastered.

A class need not be intellectually challenging in order to have a sobering impact. The damage control training, for example, was quite pedestrian in concept. A seawater leak is a bad thing and must be expeditiously repaired. Check. Damage control kits consist of various wooden plugs, wedges, and metal bands that might be used to stanch leakage from bulkheads or pipes. See a leak; plug it. Got it. The theory is obvious. A quick trip to the water tank trainer leaves a lasting impression, however. The water used for leak simulation is chlorinated potable water like that in a swimming pool. It is not oceanic saltwater. Although it is not heated, it is downright balmy compared to the temperatures one would encounter at ocean depths. And while it is pumped through the myriad practice ruptures at moderate pressure, the intensity of an actual breach at depth would be many times greater. Let the games begin.

## LEADERSHIP LESSON 6.A.
## COMMUNICATION MUST BE MULTI-CHANNEL.

The first simulated rupture in the damage control trainer is a moderately small pipe breach. In concept, the problem is obvious. What's not obvious is that water spraying from even a tiny hole enters with a deafening roar, rendering communication impossible. Now there's an unanticipated repair challenge. Even screaming at the top of our lungs, we are unable to convey even simple instructions to the sailor next to us. In the confined space typical of a submarine, the pandemonium of spraying water is deafening and confounding. And precisely where is the leak?

It is easy to see jets of water shooting from various surfaces, but which of them is the actual breach and which are ricochets? Even with ambient temperature tank water, the scene is uncomfortably chilly. Hypothermia and numb fingers when you need dexterity would clearly be real issues in the open ocean. Once we finally discern the actual leak from the many impinging water sprays, we realize that in the tight, inaccessible space, the application of the damage control wedges and bands will be anything but straightforward. As the water continues to blast at the simulated shipboard electronics cabinets and floods around our ankles, we cannot help but wonder about the safety of the equipment and the potential for electrical mishaps should this be actual saltwater in a real catastrophe. As would surely be the case in a real breach of this nature, the simulator allows the leak to grow larger with time as we continue to fumble and flounder our way through the exercise.

Just as we're feeling good about plugging the small pipe breach and finally able to hear ourselves speak again, the trainer ratchets up the challenge a few orders of magnitude by creating a simulated hull breach. The water rushing through the gaping void is formidable. This time the location of the breach is obvious, but how to plug the jagged gulf is much less so. Moving toward the leak is like forging upstream through a strong river current, the water forcing us backward every step of the way. There is no banding, clamping, or inserting a plug into this breach. Creative thinking on the fly is required. A mattress from the sleeping quarters shoved against the breach and braced with any moveable items to jam the mattress tight is enough to slow the leak; there simply will be no stopping it. Pumping the water out as best as possible while planning for proper repairs will have to do.

## LEADERSHIP LESSON 6.B.
## FIREFIGHTERS ARE TRUE HEROES.

Perhaps a simulated fire will be easier to survive. We are placed in an enclosed tank approximately the size of a typical space on a submarine, but the layout is artificially simplistic. The tank is entirely empty with free space to move in all directions, totally devoid of equipment we would normally be stumbling and tripping over in blackout conditions. At the far end of the tank is a shallow basin into which a small amount of diesel fuel will be poured and ignited. Our job will be to enter the burning space from the opposite end and to use the appropriate ship-board firefighting nozzles to fend off the heat and douse the blaze. We have at our disposal OBA, self-contained oxygen breathing apparatus, and EAB, hose-fed emergency air breathing masks to enable breathing while in the tank. What could be simpler than this? Before the blaze is ignited, we see the idle tank, observe the basin that will be set aflame, and otherwise know exactly where the fire will be and how we are to extinguish it. An actual shipboard mishap would be many times more complex than this drill.

Within seconds of the diesel fuel igniting, the visibility inside the tank drops to zero. As rapidly as visibility falls, the temperature rises. If we didn't have the four-foot-long spray applicator nozzle aimed forward above our ducked heads, the air would be hot enough to spontaneously ignite our hair, or so claim the instructors, and it feels as though they speak the truth. This is where an air-tight seal on the breathing mask literally saves lives. With sufficient advance instruction and intense oversight, we successfully beat the fire and have another lifelong experience burned into our brains. The thought of having to enter a burning space on an actual ship without prior knowledge of the fire's location, having to wind the hoses between rows of equipment in total darkness, having to locate the next EAB receptacle to plug into for another breath . . . No, thank you.

## LEADERSHIP LESSON 6.C.
## EXERCISE YOUR BRAIN.

Typical SOBC classroom instruction was much less intense. Mornings began with a few minutes of "mental gymnastics," a series of calculations performed quickly in one's head to determine basic ship-maneuvering details. Given data on our own ship course and speed with observations on another ship's bearing, relative bearing, range, or observed bow angle, it is possible to calculate the missing detail on the other ship's course. The ability to quickly determine these details is as useful in safely conning the ship during peacetime to ensure safe passage without collision as it is in setting fire-control solutions on target combatant vessels during time of war. With regular "mental gym" practice, one can determine the needed missing detail from the available data in mere seconds. As a side benefit, the exercise notably improved our basic arithmetic skills.

Much SOBC training is dedicated to conning room or ship-driving simulation activities. Many hours in cramped, dimly lit spaces listening to the equivalent of party line communications on the sound-powered phones in one ear, while simultaneously exchanging vital information with other key watchstanders with the other ear develops an exceptional capacity to multitask. The specific systems knowledge gained is, in many cases, unique to a specific ship configuration, but the more fundamental skills of clear, concise communication and focused execution in a fast-paced, high-pressure, interdisciplinary environment are readily transferable to other work situations.

## LEADERSHIP LESSON 6.D.
## LEAD PEOPLE; MANAGE THINGS.

A true gem of the SOBC experience is a course dubbed LMET, or Leadership and Management Education and Training. In typically effective military style, LMET consists of both classroom lecture and role-playing segments. The course covers the essential traits and skills of both good managers and good leaders, and outlines the difference between the two while stressing that the successful officer is competent in both areas. The course teaches management systems for tracking status of projects and programs along with priority-setting skills. Leadership skills are learned from the perspective of those who will be led; empathy with a subordinate and understanding their humanity allows the leader to more effectively motivate desired team behavior. Many people seem to confuse leadership and management, or to incorrectly use the two terms interchangeably. As one officer succinctly stated to distinguish leadership from management, "You lead people while you manage things."

## LEADERSHIP LESSONS:

**6.A.** Communication must be multi-channel. Even when working side-by-side, verbal communication became impossible in the presence of a water leak; the roar of the spraying water rendered even shouting futile. Communication can, and should, occur via multiple means. When simple verbal communication is rendered ineffective, use headsets if available, or shift instead to visual cueing. Texting or an email can serve when tele-communication becomes unavailable. A bit of advance consideration of possible conditions and planning to address issues will enable shifts in communication channels in real time.

**6.B.** Firefighters are true heroes. Entering an inferno to save others at one's own peril is the calling of a special person. Not every job or role is a suitable fit for every person. Think of the firefighter should you ever catch yourself feeling superior to someone simply due to their station in life.

**6.C.** Exercise your brain. The brain is like a muscle, growing stronger and more capable with exercise. Make a conscious effort to challenge your brain with new puzzles or problems on a regular basis.

**6.0.** Lead people; manage things. Never confuse management of assets, budgets, projects, or any inanimate object with leadership of cognizant, sentient, emotional human beings. To lead is to inspire people to perform. To manage is to measure and prioritize actions. The skills necessary for management differ markedly from those of leadership.

# PART III

# POSITIONAL LEADER

Organizations of all stripes fill leadership positions with those who exhibit conforming behavior. The determined follower is a model employee, an exemplar of traits desired by the leadership hierarchy, and therefore a likely candidate for promotion into the management career track as a positional leader. Promotion comes with the responsibility for a defined portion of the organization's activities, and the power to supervise the work of others.

Positional leaders are oftentimes given authority before they are fully ready for their new roles, and so these newly minted leaders continue to develop a personalized leadership style even while serving in that leadership role—learning by doing. In this phase of leadership development, we practice the best traits observed from other leaders who inspire us, and we shun the techniques we deem to be ill fitting, all while we learn from our own successes and setbacks to develop our individual leadership capabilities.

# 7

# FLEET ASSIGNMENT

After two full years of OCS, NPS, Prototype, and SOBC training, we finally receive orders to a genuine working command. The vast majority of the newly minted nuclear power officers are bound for fleet assignments, though a few are assigned back to prototype facilities to become instructors for the next generations moving through the training pipeline. Select others are diverted for service in the admiral's engineering corps, the track I had previously declined.

One of the many wonders of the Navy's inner workings is the role of the detailer. The detailer's ostensible function is to match the duty needs of the Navy with the desired appointments of the available personnel. In the earliest days of the indoctrination process, the recruiter had us believing that our duty assignments would be a matter of personal choice. By the time we reached OCS, we learned that our ultimate assignment would, indeed, be a personal choice—but it would be the detailer's, not our own.

Through each of the training pipeline assignments, we were reminded that superior performance would assure us of the ability to write our own orders, while mediocre performance would leave one's destiny to the whims of a detailer. In a fleet assignment, a set of orders would specify both the geographic location of the duty base and the class of ship to which one was assigned. In my case, I specified San Diego as my preferred base and a 637 class fast-attack submarine as my desired ship. Since I consistently finished each training assignment near the head of the class and there were many 637 class boats based in San Diego, I had little doubt on how my orders would read.

Never let it be said that the Navy lacks a sense of humor. My orders to a 688 class boat based in Pearl Harbor, Hawaii, matched neither my preferred base location nor my desired class of ship. I should have been happy to be assigned to service in the Pacific Ocean, which some might argue was a match of sorts. A buddy requested an East Coast assignment, remaining open to any ship platform just as long as he could be near his East Coast family. His orders were to a 637 class ship out of San Diego. Another classmate who requested an open class assignment on the West Coast found himself based in Groton, Connecticut. One has to stand in awe of the detailer's work. It must be difficult to dole out assignments in such a manner as to meticulously avoid fulfillment of every personal request.

Having never experienced the leisurely tropical paradise of Hawaii, I told myself that there were worse places to be stationed. The ship to which I had been assigned, the USS *Birmingham*, SSN695, was the pride of the Atlantic fleet and had just been transferred to the Pacific Fleet to be based in Pearl Harbor. Perhaps things would be all right after all?

My Navy-issued, one-way ticket to Honolulu on United Airlines had me arriving on Friday afternoon prior to the Monday morning I was to report for duty as ordered. The wardroom (the ship's officers) would meet me at the HNL gate to welcome me to the new command. Unsure of what to wear during travel and wanting to make a good first impression, I made the flight in my best summer white uniform, crisply pressed and blindingly bright. With the plane parked at the gate, my fellow passengers, all clad in the shorts and flip-flops of tourists, made their way up the aisle and into the floral fragrance of Honolulu's warm air. As I turned past the cockpit and toward the Jetway exit, the pilot exclaimed, "I envy your uniform! Mine helps meet the ladies, but yours is a magnet." Stepping from the plane uniformed as I was, the khaki-clad wardroom had no trouble identifying me from among the vacationers, and I quickly shook hands, made introductions, and matched pleasantries with a half dozen new teammates before we made the short drive back to the Pearl Harbor base. Slightly self-conscious about my dazzlingly white uniform amid the sea of khaki, I followed the small crowd of new friends through a gate and, before I could realize where we were, a crusty captain was shouting, "Welcome, Ensign! House round for all!" The entire venue erupted in excited chatter about the new ensign buying everyone a drink.

"Ah, geez, Jim. Remove your cover. There's a tradition—" began one of the wardroom JO's before I curtly interrupted.

"I know the tradition. I didn't know we were entering a club."

One of the naval traditions involves proper cover, or hat, etiquette. A sailor never goes out uncovered; otherwise stated, a sailor always wears a hat outdoors. Likewise, one never wears a cover indoors because the roof itself serves as a cover. The penalty for violating the no-cover policy and wearing a hat indoors is for the violating party to buy a house round, should the violation occur in a bar. The situation into which I stumbled was through the gate and under the thatched gazebo roof of an outdoor bar on the Pearl Harbor submarine base. In retrospect, it makes sense that late on a Friday afternoon in Hawaii people might gather at a bar, and an outdoor bar at that. But never having previously set foot on the base and naive to the fact that the gate we passed through would put us within the served confines of the bar, I had unwittingly been led to make a serious infraction. And there were a number of thirsty and rambunctious officers waiting to collect on this fine evening. Knowing I could not possibly afford the tab for a house round, my new wardroom graciously chipped in to cover the bill.

The first impression of my newfound wardroom team suggested that I could trust these guys to watch my back if in extremis, but I should remain alert in the interest of self-preservation. All off-duty officers showed up at the airport to welcome me to the ship, which demonstrates superb camaraderie (unless my Friday afternoon arrival just happened to present an opportune excuse to evacuate the ship for an early round of drinks at the Officers' Club).

When I got tagged with a house round for violating the no-cover-in-the-bar tradition, the guys immediately anted up to cover the bill, which none of us would have been obligated to pay had anyone thought to clue me in as to the nature of the venue. Yes, they seemed to have good intentions, but I would do well to remain vigilant.

I settled in at the BOQ (Bachelor Officers' Quarters) on the Pearl Harbor Submarine Base that first evening, awed by the floral-fragrant breeze streaming through the open window and discomforted by the warm, humid air. The BOQ room was adequate, yet too spartan to be a place anyone would want to stay for any length of time. Any sound reverberated throughout the aged building, and the lack of air-conditioning ensured no escape from the sticky air.

Security of personal belongings was another concern. The door to the BOQ room was the cheap, slatted variety typically found obscuring a household interior washing machine or water heater; any determined teenager would be able to punch through the slats without a second thought. I could not decide which was more disconcerting: the fact that I could see through the door slats as people passed in the hallway and hear every word of their conversations, or the piles of telltale wood dust and the incessant gnawing sound emanating from the wood-boring beetles inside the door that continually reminded me that the slats were growing weaker by the minute.

As luck would have it, two other bachelor officers from my same command were staying at the BOQ, and one of them was eager to find a roommate and to move off base to a civilian residence. Seizing the opportunity, I visited the Navy's relocation center for maps and rent listings, and, after a fair amount of searching and touring, we signed a lease for a high-rise condo in Aiea. From our window, we could view Pearl Harbor, Ford Island, the *Arizona* Memorial, and sunsets over the Pacific Ocean. With "home" situated, it was time to dive into work.

## LEADERSHIP LESSON 7.A.
## ANTICIPATE YOUR IMPACT ON OTHERS.

The wardroom officers comprised an interesting mix of gentlemen. Most hailed from the East Coast and were none too pleased with the *Birmingham's* change of home port and their recent relocation to the Pacific Ocean. All possessed the intellect one would expect of the nuclear training pipeline, with the exception of the supply officer, whose staff duties would never include direct line responsibility for the ship. There were three tiers of officers responsible for the ship. The first tier was our captain, the commanding officer (CO), and his right hand, the executive officer (XO). The second tier of department heads included the navigator, the engineering officer, and the weapons officer. The third tier of division officers included the junior officers, such as myself, serving their first sea tour of duty.

The CO served as a role model, albeit not of the desired nature. His abrupt demeanor left me wondering from our initial introduction what I had done to upset him. Perhaps my day-one infraction at the outdoor bar had other COs ribbing him behind closed doors at the Officers' Club? As I gained the trust and confidence of fellow officers, they shared many stories of working with our CO. He was a career Navy man who coveted the next rung of the promotion ladder, and the fact that he had twice been passed over for promotion had left a chip the size of a Los Angeles–class nuclear submarine on his shoulder without the collar insignia to match. His style was to demand respect for his rank and to bark orders, not so much to communicate operational intent as to convey his positional superiority.

During a casualty drill one day while I was standing watch as duty officer, the drill simulation team stood next to a shore power distribution cabinet waving a gray flag to simulate smoke emanating from the ship's main electrical feed. A petty officer standing duty with me observed the clue, surmised the drill to be an electrical fire within the panel, grabbed the nearest $CO_2$ fire extinguisher, and pointed the extinguisher's nozzle at the panel to simulate immediate firefighting. I reported the drill fire's location and that extinguishing efforts were in progress. At this point in a drill, one would expect the drill simulators to indicate a status change, whether the fire was growing or whether our firefighting efforts were improving the situation. In this case, however, the CO stormed angrily to the panel and screamed, "You can't use an extinguisher without direct access to the fire!" Both the petty officer and I hesitated momentarily, wondering if the CO actually wanted us to open the energized electrical cabinet feeding the ship in dry dock.

Seeing our hesitation, the CO fumbled hastily with the cabinet latch several times before yanking the electrical cabinet door wide open, then grabbing the nozzle of the extinguisher from the petty officer and thrusting it toward the base of the internal circuit breakers as way of instruction.

In his zeal to demonstrate what should have been done, the CO had torn the panel door from its track and accidentally struck the petty officer holding the extinguisher with it. Incensed at the scene, the CO directed his ire at me for not having opened that panel door to assist in fighting the drill fire. My father being the city fire marshal in my hometown, my upbringing was steeped in firefighting knowledge. I was privileged to have observed with the fire department crew the enclosed-space fire model and understood the danger of fireball expansion when a door is suddenly opened and the inrush of oxygen feeds the existing flames. I kept that knowledge to myself during this particular drill.

Later that long day, after the drill critique and after other crew members had departed, the glum petty officer who had been first to the scene with fire extinguisher in hand sought my feedback on how he might do better in the future. He clearly knew how to use an extinguisher, to pull the pin, to squeeze the handle trigger, to aim the discharge at the base of flames, and to sweep the discharge from side to side. In the heat of the drill, he had simply been concerned about whether opening the energized electrical cabinet would be entirely safe. I assured him that I had full confidence in his ability, as should he, and that the CO's anger was directed at me and not at him.

## LEADERSHIP LESSON 7.B.
## LEARN FROM OTHER LEADERS' ACTIONS, BOTH GOOD AND BAD.

Another noteworthy display of undesirable leadership from the top occurred when I requested to attend dive school. The command maintained a team of certified Navy divers whose expertise was employed to confirm conditions of the ship's hull or intake and discharge ports while it was berthed alongside the dock. The dive team knew that I had obtained scuba certification while stationed in Florida during Nuclear Power School, and they suggested that I attend dive school to become their dive leader. I appreciated the team request and naively approached the CO to ask his permission. Without pausing for even a moment to consider my request, he barked, "Why should I let you?" In a stern and perturbed tone, he ranted on about how, early in his career, he had made this same request of his CO and had been denied. The reason he gave for denying my request now was that his same request had been denied years earlier.

## LEADERSHIP LESSON 7.C.
## GIVE ONLY OF YOUR OWN TIME AND RESOURCES.

The overt effort to manage upward was perhaps the most disdainful trait of the ship's captain. I knew from experience that the Navy took care of even a lowly ensign when orders came in to transfer from one duty location to another. The Navy provided movers who would arrive at the current place of residence and wrap, pack, and transport all household goods to the new location. Given that Rank Has Its Privileges (RHIP), one can only imagine the moving services provided to an admiral. So our surprise bordered on shock when the CO informed the wardroom that our admiral, his boss, would be moving and that he had arranged for us the honor of serving as the admiral's moving crew on Saturday. Through his decades of service and foreign travel, the admiral had acquired an impressive collection of solid wood, hand-carved furniture. Our precious weekend day was dedicated to brute forcing the massive-yet-delicate furniture from upstairs rooms, down the double flight of stairs, through the house, and outdoors for transport. The strenuous weight-lifting workout was a smaller commitment than the donation of our arms, legs, and bodies as padding between furniture and walls or door jambs to ensure no nicks or scratches to the precious cargo during the extraction and moving process. Of course, the CO was present to supervise our efforts with verbal negative reinforcement should the furniture approach too close to the wall for comfort. We survived the exercise, but the favor delivered up the chain of command left little feeling of internal gratitude for a good deed done. Under other circumstances, an invitation to the big boss's home may have provided a boost to morale. As staged, it was apparent that we were mere pawns in the CO's effort to buy attention.

—————

The cast of characters who made up my colleagues in the wardroom included officers from different parts of the country, and of different educational and social backgrounds. I'll introduce them here with invented names that highlight their most prominent personality traits.

Among the wardroom division officers was Mr. Scowly, a very bright and capable IFNAG (ignorant freaking Naval Academy graduate), who served as an oracle of advice and guidance to the newest junior officers but who seemed to relish the big brother role just a bit too much. The epitome of the Navy's finest in most ways, Mr. Scowly was a brown-noser.

A bit too preoccupied with pleasing the boss, he seemed in constant peril of his own suffocation or of inflicting upon the captain a need of considerable proctologic work should the CO too suddenly stop while walking. The next most seasoned of the junior officers was Mr. Freud, a truly nice guy whose only dream in life was to be a great naval officer. Mr. Freud had graduated from Vermont Military Institute and, try as he might, he could never quite escape the shadow of Mr. Scowly, nor shake the kind, doofus image he unwittingly projected.

Then we had Mr. Real. Vertically challenged, whip smart, and sporting the glasses one might stereotypically expect of one with his credentials, Mr. Real boasted a nuclear engineering degree from Penn State even before entering the nuclear training pipeline, and without a doubt he was the most straightforward, unpretentious JO onboard.

Mr. Spiro was a painful example of how bureaucracy can affect good people. Another truly good guy, Mr. Spiro was bright and possessed an enjoyable dry wit. Some time after passing all the physical requirements and signing on for nuclear submarine duty, he was diagnosed with a lung ailment. The Navy subsequently determined Mr. Spiro to be unfit for submarine sea duty, barring him from completing the qualifications required for promotion and damning him to a life of lousy shore duty rotations.

Mr. Preppy was known to wear tennis shorts and shirt with his Sperry Topsiders when off duty, all capped off with a sweater tossed over his shoulders, the long sleeves casually crossed in front. All this just for an afternoon stroll in Waikiki. Mr. Preppy joined the Navy for the officer's uniform and the positional respect that he so desperately craved, probably knowing that he would be hard-pressed to earn respect in a less hierarchical environment.

Rounding out the wardroom were Mr. Tremble and Mr. Perky. Mr. Tremble was another Nittany Lion from Penn State whose idiosyncrasies surely inspired Matt Groening to create Barney's character on *The Simpsons*. Mr. Tremble never had a date during the years that we served together, but he could always be relied upon to release the most guttural belch at the most opportune time in the presence of mixed company. Always the ladies' man, Mr. Tremble owned and drove what may have been the only late model Chevrolet Caprice on the entire island of Oahu, and he was always willing to drive should we manage to luck into any off-duty free time.

Mr. Perky was an effervescent smiling sort during the waking periods between his narcoleptic episodes. Poor Mr. Perky could doze off during any activity, from attending a classroom lecture to standing a watch in the ship's engineering plant. Once the rest of us determined that he was not lazy but truly narcoleptic, we pulled together to cover for him as best we could.

Messrs. Tremble and Real were the most conscientious in making me feel a part of the wardroom team. They each invested time in touring me around not only every space of the ship, but also around the dry dock in which the ship was keel-blocked, the shipyard itself, the submarine base, and even the entire island of Oahu when our stars aligned on the duty roster and we had mutual off-duty time. Each knew his trade and graciously shared knowledge to accelerate my progress along the learning curve. When either of them stubbed a toe of their own in discovering a new regulatory boundary in the shipyard working environment, they shared the new knowledge to help me avoid making the same mistake.

This fine collection of gentlemen, all eager for life at sea, found themselves beached at Pearl Harbor Naval Shipyard. Only days prior to my arrival, the ship had been positioned in dry dock for a scheduled 16-month overhaul. Each of us was looking forward to completing the planned upgrades to the ship and getting back out to sea. The Navy's extensive training had prepared us well for life aboard an operating ship; no training prepared us for life on dry land in a shipyard overhaul environment.

At sea, the ship belonged to the officers and crew, and control of the vessel followed a well-defined chain of command. Positioned on keel blocks in the shipyard, the ship suddenly became less a single entity than a collection of subsystems. The shipyard personnel boarded, disassembled various subsystems, connected myriad temporary systems, and otherwise set about installing the planned upgrades. To be sure, the ship's chain of command remained in effect, but a parallel control structure was also put in place by the shipyard's civilian tradespeople. Just days before, a knowledgeable, trained, and qualified officer could make a decision, issue an order, and move smartly forward with a given undertaking. Within the confines of the shipyard, multiple trade specialties now had to be involved in any decision, and multiple independent organizations had to be briefed and reach agreement before any activity could proceed.

For the safety of personnel and equipment, constant communication of subsystem status between the naval and civilian workers was imperative. Unfortunately, the shipyard's tradespeople lacked the sense of urgency ingrained into the naval personnel. The responsible officer for any given evolution—the set of projects to be completed during the course of the ship's overhaul—was available day and night, holidays and weekends included, to promptly provide input or approval for the scheduled activities. On the other hand, it wasn't uncommon for schedules to be delayed because the shipyard's authorizing authorities couldn't be reached or because they couldn't reach agreement. The ship's crew tended to focus intently on the task at hand, working steadily and diligently until the task was satisfactorily completed. The shipyard workers, in contrast, conscientiously worked to their shift clock. Scheduled breaks were inviolate. Should a task be in process when break time drew near, the tradespeople workers would methodically prepare the affected subsystem for stasis during their scheduled break rather than continue until they had completed the task. On many occasions, the time it took to position the subsystem into a stable configuration and then to return it to the pre-break status after the break was several times longer than would have been needed to merely complete the task without interruption.

## LEADERSHIP LESSON 7.0.
## PACE THE EFFORT.

Many among the ship's crew naively believed going in that Pearl Harbor shipyard duty would be a plum assignment, that hours would be shorter than at sea, and that there would be ample time to enjoy the Hawaiian island life. Reality proved to be much harsher. A typical duty day for the military personnel began at 0700 and ran until 0800 the following day. Arriving at 0700 on the duty day would allow the crew sufficient time to tour the ship, understand the ever-changing status of the subsystems, discuss status with the offgoing crew, attend a briefing of scheduled activities for the next 24 hours, and relieve the offgoing watchstanders by 0800. Should it happen to be a Saturday or Sunday morning, when relieved of the watch, the offgoing watchstanders could go home to sleep following their 24 hours on duty. On weekdays, however, those coming off watch would resume a "normal" 10- to 12-hour shipyard workday of attending classes, processing paperwork, meeting with division personnel, and running drills. Far from the fabled civilian nine-to-five assignment, the shipyard-bound duty officer would depart home, heading for work in the morning not to return again until the following evening, some 36 hours later.

Each duty day was a grueling test of human physical and mental endurance. The fresh oncoming ship's crew arrived concurrently with the shipyard's day crew in the cool comfort of the morning air. Wearing a fresh uniform, steel-toed safety boots, hard hat, safety goggles, and earplugs, each person boarded the ship ready to seize the day. In short order, however, the cool morning topside breeze was replaced by the stifling baked air of the dry dock and the confines of the not-presently-air-conditioned ship essentially became a large, enclosed dark steel tube, uncomfortably dank and humid. The cacophony of abrasive blasting, grinding, and needle-gunning reverberated throughout the ship's hull, joined incessantly by the deafening sirens of the industrial blowers in the dry dock basin, whose purpose was to keep the foul air flowing from the stricken ship.

At 1600 (four p.m. civilian time) the spent shipyard crew feebly mounted the dry dock ladders and headed for home, their jumpers clinging to their sweaty forms, their hair matted to their soaked brows, and their faces streaked with the grist of their work. Even as the exhausted day-shift civilian workers ascended the ladders, the swing-shift workers began their descent to take up where their day-working brethren left off. While the civilian workers rotated in a separate crew every eight hours in dayshift, swing shift, and midnight or graveyard shift succession, the Navy's crew remained on duty for a full 24 hours. The enlisted men would rotate watch-standing duties during their 24-hour duty period, but there was no such relief for the duty officers; they remained vigilant for the full duration.

Depending upon the evolutions in progress during any given grave-yard shift, the duty officer might occasionally attempt to catch a few minutes of sleep. Given the state of exhaustion experienced by 0100, some 17 hours into the marathon workday, it might by physically possible to doze for a few fitful minutes amid the deafening ruckus and despite the stifling heat and humidity inside the sunbaked cylinder. Personal experience showed that roughly 20 minutes of shut-eye were possible between requests for hot-work authorization, work order approval, or other calls of duty. I never could decide which left me more exhausted, going the full 24 hours with no attempt at sleep whatsoever or having 20-minute segments of semiconsciousness before being rousted back to duty.

## LEADERSHIP LESSON 7.E.
## NEVER CONFUSE "PEOPLE" FOR "RESOURCES."

A typical week would start Sunday morning at 0600 when I would rise for a quick shower, shave, and a bite to eat before heading to the shipyard to begin the system status checks by 0700 in preparation for relieving the watch by 0800. On duty by 0800 Sunday morning, there were 24 hours of engine room preventive maintenance to complete until 0800 Monday morning, when another officer would officially relieve me of the watch. At 0800 Monday morning, having already logged 25 hours at work for the week, I would report to the ship's barge for muster, provide the CO with an offgoing watch report, maybe slip in a quick shower and change of uniform if time permitted, and undertake my divisional and collateral duties for the day. Being a typical, nonduty day, on Mondays I could generally wrap things up by 1800 before heading home. On many occasions I logged 40 hours of work for the new week by Monday evening!

In a worst-case scenario, the duty officers would be on a port and starboard watch rotation, meaning that every other day was a duty day. During port and starboard periods, I would be heading back to work Tuesday morning, not for a standard 10- to 12-hour workday but for another 24-hour duty day, followed by the standard day on Wednesday. Depending upon the duty cycle and availability of other qualified officers, I routinely logged 100-hour workweeks and multiple weeks of 120 hours when fellow officers found themselves disqualified to stand watch for various infractions and citations. Being the most junior qualified officer assigned to the ship, I was virtually assured of weekend duty. I pulled more than three straight months of Sunday duty before politely approaching the navigation officer who wrote the ship's duty schedule. "Nav, not sure you're aware, but I've stood duty on Sunday for three solid months."

"Really?" he said quizzically. "I'll look at the schedule." And so he did. After voicing this observation (i.e., complaining), he assigned me exactly one duty-free weekend before making me a permanent fixture on the Saturday duty roster.

## LEADERSHIP LESSON 7.F.
## KEEP LIFE'S PRIORITIES STRAIGHT.

Given the intensity of the work environment and the horrendous hours, personal and family life was forced into a secondary role. Some of the saltiest, most tenured chiefs declared that a man could marry but one bride, and for a true sailor that one was the sea. Whether they truly believed this or just clung to the trite phrase to salve the wounds of failed relationships is for the psychiatrists to determine, but more than half of the junior officers who were married when assigned to the command were single by the time they left.

Of those still married by the end of the JO tour, none had the outward appearance of someone in a happy relationship. Though terrible to think, one might speculate that convenience was the glue holding the union together and that they shared the unspeakable comfort of knowing that when sea duty called again, they would enjoy up to six months of separation.

## LEADERSHIP LESSON 7.G.
## COMBAT COMPLACENCY.

Compounding the difficulty of standing a good watch in the trying environment of the shipyard were the mental challenges one faced on a daily basis. Performing abnormal breaches and modifications to the myriad nuclear reactor plant subsystems kept the adrenaline surging with each double-checked order given.

What could go wrong when we do this? What indications should we see? What action would we take should the indications be other than expected? The self-induced pressure of ensuring that there could be absolutely no opportunity for anything to go awry filled my mind with constant questions.

## LEADERSHIP LESSON 7.H.
## CONFIRM INTELLECTUAL, PHYSICAL,
## AND EMOTIONAL WELL-BEING.

As if these pressures were not enough to unnerve even the most competent, fit, and self-assured officer, the Naval Reactors Regional Office (NRRO) representatives freely roamed the shipyard and randomly dropped in for observations and audits. The intent of the NRRO visits was to provide yet another set of eyes to ensure safe execution of the myriad nuclear reactor plant activities. Unfortunately, should the NRRO representative deem anything questionable, the result would be a formal write-up of the command that would likely lead to disqualification of the watchstander(s) involved—a result that was all too common. Under these trying circumstances, paranoia ran high.

Suffering the humiliation of disqualification was yet another little shipyard mind game. The disqualified officer suffered the mental anguish of having failed to perform to the highest standard and was made to suffer the indignity of retraining, retesting, requalifying, and otherwise proving anew his fitness to stand duty. Even while suffering through this requalifying period, however, the disqualified watchstander could breathe a little freer and sleep a little more soundly knowing that he could not issue the order that might jeopardize the ship and crew, that nothing could go wrong on the watch that he would not be standing! In a perverse way, the punishment of disqualification actually might be seen as a reward. Then again, sitting on the sidelines leaves the disqualified officer with a healthy dollop of guilt for leaving fellow officers with a short duty roster rotation, thereby compounding their already grueling life of shipyard service. This sense of guilt only serves to foment with the anguish of failure and perverse sense of duty-relief already preying upon a sidelined officer's sanity.

## LEADERSHIP LESSON 7.1.
## UNDERSTAND THE READINESS PERIOD.

Given the intense intellectual, emotional, and physical demands of the nuclear shipyard environment, it seemed nearly inevitable that some disqualifying infraction, no matter how minor, would occur on a given officer's watch. Indeed, nearly every officer who regularly served on the engineering duty officer watch rotation at one point or another found himself disqualified (DQ'd). Some officers such as Mr. Preppy, Mr. Tremble, and Mr. Perky were familiar fixtures on the DQ list, and when we reviewed the disqualifying events, we would collectively agree that the infractions were avoidable. When the likes of Mr. Spiro or Mr. Real found themselves disqualified, however, we would often learn some unforeseen subtlety of the temporary subsystems and the shipyard would end up modifying procedures to ensure the next ship would learn from the documented-protocol omission.

During one spate of abnormally high DQs among the wardroom officers, the CO assembled us inside a makeshift conference room on the barge and asked our thoughts on why we were having so many infractions. He went methodically around the room, asking each of us in turn for our causal assessment. We each voiced our opinions, which covered every conceivable factor as to why the environment, the shipyard, the weather, the work hours, NRRO representative personality, ambiguity of temporary-systems procedures, and any number of other problems might be the causes of our errors. When it was my turn to speak, I suggested complacency as our issue. Perhaps we were not staying fully attentive to the ever-changing situation and were allowing ourselves to lull along rather than staying sharp? Fellow officers promptly dismissed complacency as a factor, and the hunt for causes continued. When he had had his fill of this session, the CO said he would leave us to determine the root cause, that none of us were to leave the room until we had reached consensus. And with that he departed, closing the door behind him.

We continued to banter among ourselves and to offer even more remote excuses for our lapses than anyone would have offered in the CO's presence. The more we talked, the more the tone of the discussion became a gripe session about how we were victims of the circumstances. After some time, the CO returned to check our progress. He listened briefly before again departing, reminding us that we were not leaving the room until we had identified the root cause. I could not help but state an observation that all the causes being suggested were external, that we were not taking ownership for the situation. This gave some of the others pause, but ownership for the situation was clearly going to be difficult for others to accept. By the time the CO returned a second time, we had finally coalesced around complacency as the issue, an assessment the CO accepted.

## LEADERSHIP LESSON 7.J.
## RESPECT AND APPRECIATE SUBORDINATES.

On one occasion following the disqualification of Mr. Preppy, I asked one of the highly qualified petty officers who had also been on duty at the time, "How did that valve mispositioning happen? Couldn't you see the order was out of sequence?"

"We knew Mr. Preppy gave the wrong order but thought that carrying it out might teach him a lesson," was the petty officer's astonishing reply.

The bright and capable enlisted crew could have prevented the infraction. They could see the events unfolding and could have offered Mr. Preppy a suggestion to avert the infraction entirely. But the crew on duty at the time instead deemed Mr. Preppy to be such an insufferably pompous jerk that when he issued the troublesome order, they were only too willing to carry it out. They resented serving under him so much that instead of doing what they knew to be proper, they opted to do exactly as he had ordered and let him live with the consequences.

## LEADERSHIP LESSON 7.K.
## EARN RESPECT, NEVER DEMAND IT.

Being experts on the subsystems and plant status, the crew knew that no damage would come to the ship or themselves, and they took the opportunity to pay Mr. Preppy back for his demeaning arrogance by carrying out his order exactly as issued, rather than doing as they knew he had intended. There is even a name for such a response to an issued order: "malicious compliance."

## LEADERSHIP LESSON 7.L.
## BE VULNERABLE.

Such troubling situations clearly could and should have been averted. Each duty shift had assigned petty officers who were experts in reactor plant operation, electrical plant operation, machinery operation, or chemistry and radiological controls. Having a complementary team of these trained specialists led by the officer trained to be the orchestrating generalist should have provided for safe execution of any approved procedure. Malicious compliance clearly throws a wrench in this carefully planned and implemented double-control strategy.

The troubling thing about a case of malicious compliance is that someone is consciously choosing to perform wrongly. The person or team committing the offending act has the training, experience, and intelligence to know that the order received is not the one intended, but also the knowledge that their actions are defensible since they were, quite literally, carrying out the letter of an order from a superior officer. In actual practice, malicious compliance is a rare event, and within a functional team built upon mutual trust and respect, such an event would never occur. My own record is evidence to that. During my three years of watchstanding in a shipyard environment, no reportable incident ever occurred on my watch. I can assure you that this record had far less to do with my watchstanding prowess than with solid crew teamwork—the kind that is only possible with mutual trust and respect. On a number of occasions, an enlisted man would hesitate prior to carrying out an issued order to give me time to rethink what I had just said. If the silent pause had not brought me to catch my own misstep, he might politely request clarification on an issued order, or otherwise ask if I had perhaps meant for a slightly different operation to be performed. Through solid teamwork, it was possible for the team to perform flawlessly even when a teammate occasionally erred.

## LEADERSHIP LESSONS:

**7.A.** Anticipate your impact on others. Consider ahead of time the impact of your actions and words on others, especially your subordinates.

During his passionate critique of our firefighting skills, the CO mortified the petty officer and had me suppressing a strong urge to shout disparaging comments about his parentage. Despite his good intentions for an improved performance outcome, the boss unwittingly inspired the opposite with his actions and words.

**7.B.** Learn from other leaders' actions, both good and bad. Many books on leadership theory describe the positive traits of a superb leader. Such material is helpful but insufficient. What's missing in many of these primers is overt statement of undesirable leadership traits to avoid.

Make note of what types of leadership actions fail and which succeed. Take note of the impact certain leaders' actions and decisions have on your outlook and motivation throughout your career, and pay forward the positive. As for the negative, let those serve as lessons of actions to avoid, and then keep them as memories in your past.

By denying my request to attend Navy diver school, the CO lowered the morale of not only one person but of an entire team. The request that I attend diver school had come from the ship's enlisted divers; they wanted me to join as their leader. Approving this minor request would have bolstered the morale of these men and demonstrated an appreciation for their input and trust in their judgment. Instead, not only did the CO's decision disappoint me, but the diver team morale lost the boost of what could have been an easy win.

**7.C.** Give only of your own time and resources. Respect the time and resources of others. Rather than committing the free time of his subordinates to "volunteer" as a weekend moving party for his superior, the boss could have floated the idea past us in advance. "Would anyone like to meet the big boss this weekend? I'm putting together a team to help him move, and I'm sure he would appreciate and remember the favor." Chances are that some of us would have actually volunteered if approached in this manner. Give freely of what is yours. Never offer the time or resources of others without their prior consent.

**7.D.** Pace the effort. The human mind and body can endure far more than the typical person would willingly undergo. Never test human limits over a prolonged period. If a situation requires a short burst of extreme effort, make the sprint. But do not allow such behavior to become the norm. Just as trying to sprint the distance of a marathon will end in failure, pushing too hard for too long at work will end in burnout and suboptimal performance.

**7.E.** Never confuse "people" for "resources." People are individual human beings worthy of common courtesy and respect, never to be treated as mundane assets or inanimate objects. Put conscious effort into the human considerations when doling out assignments. Yes, humans are resources that can accomplish great things, but they are not resources in the sense of machinery, equipment, or financial assets that are deployed without consideration of an actual life outside of work.

**7.F.** Keep life's priorities straight. Family or personal life comes first, work or career comes second, self-improvement or continuing educational pursuits come third, and leisure or solitary time rounds out the list. Many people with ambition never realize they have the order of their first two priorities confused until it is too late, and all too frequently the third priority is overlooked entirely.

**7.G.** Combat complacency. It is human nature to become habituated to our routines. We readily adapt from that nervous two-handed grip on the steering wheel, white-knuckling our way through our first rush-hour traffic drive, to that one casual hand on the wheel with the other hand cradling a smartphone, texting or scrolling through the same driving circumstances. To avoid becoming complacent, put forth conscious thought to your situation.

Anticipate what you expect to happen. I literally challenge myself to consider not only what would be the desired outcome but what could possibly go awry. Consider what would be the earliest indications that something is going awry. Plan what action you would take to mitigate or correct course away from an undesired outcome and toward the desired outcome. By taking the time to anticipate, consider, and plan in advance, it is possible to avoid the ill effects of complacency in professional and personal settings.

**7.H.** Confirm intellectual, physical, and emotional well-being. The enlightened leader considers both the collective team's capabilities and individual team members' intellectual, physical, and emotional well-being when forming plans and making individual assignments. In the pressure cooker environment of the nuclear reactor plant undergoing massive equipment and systems upgrades, the grueling hours combined with the intense scrutiny under the watchful eyes of auditors led even the best of the officers to make mistakes. Pay attention to team well-being, both at the individual and collective level, and call a pause to the action when needed to relieve pressure.

**7.I.** Understand the readiness period. At times we must wait until others are ready to move forward, and meanwhile do our best to encourage and prepare them to do so. In our team's search for the root cause of recent DQs, I knew complacency was our collective issue, yet the others were not yet ready for that answer when I first voiced it. Rather than allowing the subject to be moved aside before bringing it up again hours later, I could have probed for their thoughts and led a discussion on why they believed complacency to be a nonissue. People need to move along at a pace comfortable to them—to try to rush or pressure them can incite fierce resistance—but with conscious effort, you can help others to more quickly reach their readiness period when they will be receptive to change.

**7.J.** Respect and appreciate subordinates. Those who are at your service, if taken for granted, can readily educate the positional superior on the finer points of power flow. Treat each team member as a valued contributor, give them kudos for a job well done, and show them respect for their work and thoughts. Seek—and graciously accept—their feedback on how you might improve as the team leader.

**7.K.** Earn respect, never demand it. Resist the temptation to issue an order simply because the organizational hierarchy indicates that you can. Show through your words and actions that you are human, just like the rest. Speak with team members as colleagues, not as subordinates. Coordinated teamwork is necessary for success. If a superior does not recalibrate a leader who would abuse his positional power, a wise subordinate likely will.

**7.L.** Be vulnerable. By admitting that I did not know all the answers and by showing the crew that I respected and valued their input, the team pulled together to produce outstanding results. The secret to "my" success was to openly engage the crew as individuals and as a team to carry out the plan of the day. I regularly solicited the team's input and integrated their feedback into our activities. I also did not pretend to be faultless, and there were many opportunities for malicious compliance during my time standing watch. Still, the crew understood the intent of my orders and worked with me and one another to ensure our collective success. By making myself vulnerable, the crew and I established mutual trust and respect. Simply stated, we had each other's back.

# 8

# PEARL HARBOR
# NAVAL SHIPYARD

### LEADERSHIP LESSON 8.A.
### LEARN THE HISTORY OF YOUR COMPANY.

The workings of a shipyard are an amazing testament to human industrial capability. To witness the massive tons of steel dangling from immense cranes being manipulated into precise position amid the roar of the omnipresent machinery and flashes of the welders' arcs, one can only ponder in awe how this dance ever came to be. Pearl Harbor Naval Shipyard (PHNSY) has not only the machinery, the tradespeople, and the activity one would expect of such a storied establishment, but it also has a place in history that every child since the class of 1941 has studied in detail.

The cranes of PHNSY at the time of my arrival were the very same ones in service on December 7, 1941. How did they survive the bombardment? To hear the bells ring as they rumble into motion along their tracks, to watch their improbably huge booms swing into position, in my mind's eye I am transported back in time to my undergraduate engineering statics and dynamics courses. The calculations of the compressive and tensile forces carried along the cranes' structural members represented a substantial challenge to solve with digital computers. Those who came decades before performed these calculations with slide rules and pencils. What an inspiring feat! The motto of PHNSY, "No Ka Oi," was emblazoned on the facades of the most visible buildings. In Hawaiian this means "the best" or "number one," and at first thought it seems a fitting declaration.

Visible in Pearl Harbor across from the shipyard sits Ford Island and the USS *Arizona* Memorial, the most infamous landmark. Access to Ford Island for training classes was via "foot ferries," small boats operated by the Navy's boatswain's mates (bosuns, in casual parlance). The bosuns, both male and female, each exhibited deft handling skills in maneuvering the small boats to precise landings despite wind or water conditions. The *Arizona* Memorial, straddling the sunken battleship, remains a hallowed location that evokes introspection, as small droplets of oil—"the tears of the *Arizona*"—periodically float to the surface. When immersed in present-day frenetic activity, it is all too easy to forget the history of what made us great in the first place.

## LEADERSHIP LESSON 8.B.
## CONSIDER YOUR IMPACT ON
## THE COMPANY'S REPUTATION.

The overhaul of the USS *Birmingham* at PHNSY was scheduled for sixteen months from start to finish. The schedule of planned work accounted for all known repair and retrofit activity. Unfortunately, the tradespeople of PHNSY slipped into a daily mode of punching a time clock, and the focus became the hourly cadence of another workday with too little attention paid to quality or efficiency. Delays soon began to cascade, and none of the people responsible seemed to care. The attitude seemed to be what doesn't get done on this shift will get done on the next one.

The shipyard work ethic seemed to mirror the tropical island vibe, relaxed and unhurried. Tensions between us and them mounted as the ship's crew pushed to complete not only the plan of the day but also makeup for the previous day's progress shortfalls, while the tradespeople maintained standard pace through an eight-hour shift. One of the ship's duty officers once happened upon a tradesperson asleep on the job, nudged him back to wakefulness, and encouraged him to get back to work. When the same tradesperson was discovered sleeping on the job again a few days later, the duty officer reported the issue to the sleeper's supervisor. Incredulously, the supervisor claimed that the worker had not been asleep at all but focused intently on his work, which the duty officer had mistaken for slumber. The third time the same worker was found asleep rather than working, the duty officer unclipped the man's badge from his coveralls and took it up the shipyard's chain of command as proof of the sleeping infraction. Faced with hard evidence of the sleeper's guilt, or so thought the duty officer, the tradespeople claimed their worker had lost his badge that day and thanked the duty officer for finding and returning it! At this point, the PHNSY motto of Na Ka Oi came to be known by the ship's crew to mean No Can Do.

## LEADERSHIP LESSON 8.C.
## ENGAGE WORKERS IN ACTION PLANNING.

To be fair, the PHNSY workforce was much like any other. There were capable, dedicated workers on the roster who put in an honest day's work and took pride in their trade. There were also slackers whose primary concern seemed to be collecting a paycheck while doing as little actual work as possible. Management objectives may have been the root cause of the situation rather than worker laziness. When workers are paid by the hour, there may be no reason to complete work in a timely manner, nor to do a quality job since slow work or the need to redo work of substandard quality results in more hours and more pay. Workers need balanced incentives.

## LEADERSHIP LESSON 8.0.
## MAKE SAFETY THE #1 PRIORITY.

The noise pollution in a shipyard dry dock is astounding. The whine of fast-spinning fan motors competes with the thrum of gigantic impellers moving thousands of cubic feet of air per minute, the vibrations of which can be felt throughout your body. The tradespeople's tools are nearly all powered by pressurized air, and air hoses snake through all spaces and passageways of the ship, some strung overhead, some along gangways. All have leaks that hiss continuously, but the leaks are only noticeable during work breaks when all other cacophony subsides into the mere annoying hisses of the escaping air. While work is going on, the hissing of leaks is lost in the resonant buzz of the needle guns, the screech of the grinders, the growl of the abrasive blasters, the roar of the cutting torches, the angry zap of the welders, the whirring raps of the impact wrenches . . . The very form of the dry dock—an enormous box of concrete walls, a concrete floor, and an open-air top—is a veritable echo canyon. Dropping any metal object will fill the dry dock box with a flinch-inducing resonant clang! Communication is difficult to impossible depending upon one's location. By the end of each shift, the crews' voices are hoarse from shouting and their ears are ringing as if they had been standing a bit too close to the loudspeakers at a heavy metal concert. Enduring this noise pollution every day, all day, for months on end takes a toll.

The air pollution within the confines of a ship undergoing overhaul is also remarkable. Early in the overhaul process, the air is befouled with the burn-residue particulates of paint from cutting and grinding openings in the hull. As work progresses, the airborne particulate count increases from needle-gunning, wire-wheeling, and abrasive grinding operations that emit both physical bits of substrate material and burned residues from the generated heat. Such surface preparatory work is conducted in controlled spaces in parallel with "hot work" metal welding in other spaces. After the bulkheads, piping, and fittings are demolished to provide access to systems undergoing overhaul, the process occurs in reverse as the removed structures are welded back into place. After the hot work is completed, the work transitions to surface finishing, which involves the applications of myriad surface preparatory chemicals, sealers, primers, adhesives, and countless coats of paints. For months on end the air is foul with the many outgassing chemicals. Masks and appropriate respiratory equipment are available, of course, to protect lungs and airways. There is no such protection for the cotton uniforms, however.

The odors so thoroughly permeate the fibers of clothing that even after repeated washings, the uniforms worn in this environment retain the indescribable funk.

## LEADERSHIP LESSON 8.E.
## PICK YOUR BATTLES AND THE
## TIMING OF A CONFRONTATION.

Certain planned evolutions were sufficiently complex as to necessitate specific education and training prior to their execution. In such instances, the civilian workers and military crew members alike would attend classroom training in one of PHNSY's historical buildings. Such a session was scheduled at 0800 one morning in a classroom some 10 minutes' walk from the dry-docked ship. The rotation cycle of the schedule had me standing duty the day prior to the planned 0800 training. By the time the oncoming duty officer completed his watch preparations and said those magic words, "I relieve you," and I gave him the formal response, "I stand relieved," the clock read exactly 0800. Tired from the 24 hours on duty and coated with grime and dried sweat from the prior day's watch, my top desire was to take a warm shower. But the shower would have to wait. Duty called, and I briskly strode to the designated building to attend the scheduled class. The Pearl Harbor morning sun was already warm, and the typical humidity had again moistened my uniform by the time I reached the building and climbed the stairs up to the classroom, taking them two at a time. Conscious not to interrupt the roll call in progress,

I opened the door in the stealthy style of a submariner and eyed an open seat at the back of the room as I quietly shut the door.

Before I could reach the intended chair, the civilian instructor stopped taking attendance to challenge my presence in the room. "This is a closed session."

"I understand," I responded, meeting his eyes and motioning toward the intended open seat.

"It's 8:07. The class began at 8:00 and is closed to late entrants," he challenged with voice rising.

"I was just relieved from duty seven minutes ago and hustled here as quickly as possible. Please continue roll call while I take this seat," I offered while moving toward the chair.

"You're disrupting class and I cannot continue until you leave!" His shouting now held the rapt attention of the entire room.

The only thing I had missed was his reading the names of class participants, and I already knew my crewmates. I briefly considered the absurdity of the situation as the dozens of punctual students now turned in their seats to see how I would next respond. I decided that an open confrontation would not be conducive to classroom learning, that one verbal volley had been enough, and that a warm shower would be a better way to start the day.

Back at the ship's barge in the harbor adjacent to our dry-docked ship a few minutes later, the engineering officer observed me coming on board and reminded me of the 0800 training. I summarized for him the prior 20 minutes of my morning, and upon learning that I had been denied participation in the training session, he launched into a lecture. "You are a commissioned naval officer, and no civilian instructor should be allowed to control your actions!"

He berated me for not taking a seat in the classroom and simply refusing to budge until the instructor gave in and noted my attendance on the training attendance record. I listened quietly while he said his piece. Had I been in the mood for an argument, I would have pointed out to him that an open confrontation in front of the crew and a few civilian ship-yard workers present would not have been in keeping with the standards of military bearing as I understood them.

## LEADERSHIP LESSON 8.F.
## RESPECT YOUR POSITIONAL POWER.

I also knew something that the civilian instructor did not, which was that I was to be an instrumental participant in the evolution to be conducted. Without my availability to lead one of the scheduled shifts, there would be too few qualified engineering duty officers to complete the work. The engineering officer knew this, and I attributed his demeanor, actions, and statements to me that morning to being an emotional response brought on by realizing yet another schedule problem had surfaced. It is not clear how the communication took place, or who delivered the message to the instructor, but two days later he politely conducted a small makeup session for me and a few others.

## LEADERSHIP LESSON 8.G.
## QUESTION "THE FACTS."

The electrical power circuit breakers aboard a ship bear no resemblance to those most people know from their home breaker boxes. Only by visiting an electrical power station might you find a similar breaker, which has a form factor akin to a home refrigerator and that carries hundreds of volts in three phases rated at thousands of amperes. These vital monsters aboard a submarine are remotely operated from within the maneuvering room, the control center for the entire engine room. A simple hand switch sends a control signal to a motor inside the power breaker to open and shut its electrical contacts. The wear and tear of switching power of such magnitude gives these power circuit breakers a limited life, and they are a key focus area for refurbishment during a ship's overhaul. I was standing watch as engineering duty officer one day when a power distribution bus fed by such a breaker after its overhaul was scheduled to be reenergized for the first time. Appreciating the magnitude of the power and energy involved should anything go awry, I stationed a petty officer at the circuit breaker in addition to the electrician's mate who would remotely operate the breaker from the maneuvering room.

Upon my order to shut the breaker, which would energize the bus for the first time in many months, the electrical operator turned the breaker's remote-control switch to the shut position. A huge current surge was indicated on the electrical panel's ammeter, and the breaker's position signal on the electrical operator's panel in maneuvering showed that the breaker remained open rather than shutting as expected. The electrical operator saw the breaker's open position signal and reached to repeat the shut attempt. I asked that he wait while I phoned the petty officer stationed at the breaker to inquire what he had observed. At the power circuit breaker itself, there had been the sound of the internal motor operating to move the breaker contacts: a momentary loud hum and a heavy thud. All the information suggested that the circuit breaker had cycled shut and immediately popped open again, as if tripping open on an overcurrent condition. Two plausible scenarios for this situation came to mind: the circuit breaker refurbishment may have been of poor quality or there may have been an electrical fault (i.e., a short circuit) on the power bus fed by the breaker.

I called for a stand-down from the planned activity and reported the incident to the ship's engineering officer and to the shipyard management personnel. After confirming overall electrical plant status and then locking out and tagging out the affected power bus and circuit breaker, we opened the circuit breaker's cabinet to investigate. The problem was obvious. Rather than each of the three power phase cables being connected to their respective nodes on the circuit breaker, each of the three cables and the neutral cable were bolted to the neutral bar! All shipyard overhaul progress came to an abrupt halt pending full incident review-board investigation.

The incident review board process thoroughly interrogated everyone involved and all documented records of that circuit breaker's lifetime pedigree, including its reinstallation aboard the ship. Each of us who stood watch the day of the incident provided written statements of our actions and observations. During the closed-door incident review, the interrogations probed the preparatory steps taken prior to attempting to energize the power bus, who had approved/applied/removed the locks and tags, who was positioned where during the breaker closure attempt, what orders were given, what actions were taken, what each person saw, heard, and said. Nothing on a nuclear submarine is informal or casual. Multiple tradespeople had been involved in the breaker's reinstallation. Not only had the proper connections of power cables been confirmed independently by a separate worker, but the applied torque of each connecting bolt had been independently verified. Two people separately put torque wrench to bolt to confirm proper tightness. The ship's crew had subsequently confirmed proper installation prior to removing the LOTO locks and tags. Through these many touches and confirmations, no one had noticed that all four cables were grossly miswired to the same electrical bus rather than to their respective nodes on the breaker.

## LEADERSHIP LESSON 8.H.
## ASSESS THE SITUATION.

"Why did you station the petty office at the breaker?" "What were you thinking at the time?" These questions somehow became a prime focus of inquisition. There was nearly as much interrogation into this point as there was into how three phases of feed power came to be grotesquely and erroneously fastened to neutral. No written procedure specifies to station an observer at the breaker; it was not standard protocol. Qualified officers more senior than I said they would not have stationed someone at the breaker; the thought to do so would never have occurred to them. Our civilian counterparts concurred; it was novel and unexpected to position an observer at the breaker to be energized. Having that petty officer's observations helped inform the situation and avoided an immediate reattempt to shut the breaker, which could well have caused substantial equipment damage and overheated the conductors enough to ignite an electrical fire. Considering the hundreds of volts, the thousands of amperes, the first time energizing an electrical power bus after massive intrusion to most components and connections over a period of years in the shipyard, to me stationing the extra petty officer at the breaker had seemed like a good idea.

## LEADERSHIP LESSON 8.1.
## SOLICIT VOLUNTEERS FOR UNDESIRABLE DUTY.

As the shipyard overhaul schedule dragged on, the morale of the ship's crew sagged. The very elements that make Oahu a preferred vacation destination make it a challenging work locale. The bright sun, the ever-present warmth, and the tropical winds that make relaxing on a beach or in a hammock between swaying palm trees so enticing all make for a suboptimal work environment. The daily afternoon rains keep humidity perpetually high, and even low-intensity movement initiates perspiration. Add to the vacation-paradise setting the work environment hazards of a nuclear-powered warship. Moving about the ship in dry dock, climbing and descending ladders to reach any of the required work stations causes sweat-soaked uniforms to cling in a most uncomfortable fashion. The prescribed personal safety equipment—hard hat, goggles, ear plugs, and radiation dosimeter—add to the physical and mental burden. It takes strong mental discipline for the seagoing crew to bear a 16-month assignment to a dry dock, and the sharp curtailment to one's sense of adventure can induce island fever. The knowledge that Waikiki is but a short drive from PHNSY adds more mental burden than relief; the limited "liberty call" free time away from watchstanding duty leads to tantalizing frustration that one is placed in paradise only to toil long hours toward utter exhaustion on work that could be conducted in much less enticing geographic locations.

# LEADERSHIP LESSONS:

**8.A.** Learn the history of your company. Take pride in the accomplishments of those who came before you when building upon the foundation they set for future success.

**8.B.** Consider your impact on the company's reputation. Your actions reflect upon the company. Strive to defend your workers when possible, but acknowledge reality, apologize, and take ownership by showing corrective actions when a member of your team errs.

In the case of the sleeping shipyard worker, the management would have been far better served by acknowledging the situation, committing to investigating the matter, and then doing so. They need not have shared confidential details of the particular person's reasons for sleeping on the job. They could have suggested that all supervisors check in with their team to ensure workers are arriving for their shifts alert and well rested, and taken appropriate actions based upon their findings.

**8.C.** Engage workers in action planning. Doing so will limit their exposure to undesirable environments. It may well not be feasible to eliminate all hazards in the work environment, but soliciting volunteers or providing incentives to take on collateral-duty work can help workers feel valued. Rotate shifts to manage individual exposure.

**8.D.** Make safety the #1 priority. Ensure personnel have the right personal protective equipment (PPE) for each task and are properly trained in its use.

**8.E.** Pick your battles and the timing of a confrontation. It is wiser to rise above the moment of the situation than to let emotions fuel a confrontation. Consider the impact that your actions have on those around you. Neither subordinates nor superiors are likely to be impressed by you launching into a shouting match. Subordinates need not learn to worry about approaching you for fear of triggering an outburst, and what value is there in causing the higher-ups to doubt your ability to calmly lead in a time of crisis? Rising above the moment and demonstrating calmness that defuses a tense situation is the far better choice.

**8.F.** Respect your positional power. At the same time, remain vigilant to never abuse it.

In the case of the power-hungry instructor refusing me entry to the class, I could have informed him of my status on the spot. This might have led him to rethink his initial stance and allow me to take a seat. But the risk of a public disagreement, with him insisting even more angrily that I depart, was high. I believe my course of action to have been the more prudent under the circumstances. Walking away allowed time for emotions to clear prior to his reconvened makeup class session.

**8.G.** Question "the facts." Confirm status yourself, not to doubt the work of others but to serve as a backup to others and to add your personal integrity to the situation.

In the case of the horribly miswired circuit breaker, it is clear in hindsight that the worker who initially bolted the power feeds either was distracted while doing the work or was incompetent. Those who followed to confirm the work integrity were simply going through the motions; they added no value whatsoever. I would go so far as to say they added negative value. Rather than catching the mistake and calling for it to be fixed, their "confirmation" only served to move an error on down the line.

**8.H.** Assess the situation. Ask yourself, "What could go wrong when I do this?" Asking myself this question led to my request to have another person stationed at the circuit breaker. High voltage, high current, many variables since the bus had last been energized—the situation was too important to just plow ahead without extra attention. Consider actions you could take that would mitigate the potential issues and take action appropriate to the situation.

**8.1.** Solicit volunteers for undesirable duty. Provide incentives for team members to complete unsavory but necessary work. Even so, you may well find no one volunteers and have to assign people to challenging work. In those cases, share the load; keep durations of undesired duty brief.

# 9

# LEMON LOT

## LEADERSHIP LESSON 9.A.
## LEVERAGE EXISTING BUSINESS
## ASSETS TO BOOST TEAM MORALE.

The island of Oahu, Hawaii, represents a strategic military location in the Pacific Ocean. The US Army, Navy, Air Force, Marines, and Coast Guard each have substantial presence on Oahu, and the constant duty rotation of military members to and from bases located there makes for a vibrant used-car market. To ship a vehicle from the continental US to Hawaii when being deployed to Oahu is expensive, and the reverse shipment from Hawaii to the next destination upon completion of Oahu duties makes the proposition of bringing a personal vehicle cost prohibitive. To buy a new car on the island is also a suboptimal financial decision. The vehicle will spend most of the time sitting in tropical sun and humidity that accelerate its value depreciation while the service member tends to duty. In the end, the optimal choice for many service members is to buy a used car while on the island and to sell it again when departing.

Although Oahu's used-car market was on par with that found in most other communities, Hickam Air Force Base recognized the distinct needs of the ever-rotating military population and set aside a back parking lot for the exchange of used vehicles among military members. Abutting Pearl Harbor Naval Base and available to members of all military branches, this Hickam AFB lot was affectionately known as the Lemon Lot. Parking and display of vehicles for sale was free of charge. Sellers parked their vehicles with basic statistics of interest, asking price, and contact information taped inside the windows. Potential buyers walked the lot, identified vehicles of interest, and contacted the seller. Located on a military base, the Lemon Lot was a safe, secure, practical, and convenient solution to transportation needs of both incoming and outgoing military service members. Plus, there were no sales or commission fees.

## LEADERSHIP LESSON 9.B.
## BE HONEST IN YOUR DEALINGS WITH OTHERS.

One of the *Birmingham*'s department heads who was due for a permanent change of station (PCS) rotation drove a Fiat Spider. He knew that I was carless, and whenever I happened to be nearby, he casually spoke about how fun it was to drive the Spider. He would extol the virtues of that sporty convertible: "Nothing compares to the thrill of wind in your hair while cruising with the top down." "Every young person needs to drive a sports car before starting a family." "Hawaii is the perfect place to own a convertible." His ongoing pitches were having an effect and I was considering his ask of $2,000 for his car when another JO suggested I swing by the Lemon Lot to have a look. There was everything on the lot from 4x4 trucks to luxury cars and a station wagon. There may have been a jalopy or two, but the Lemon Lot name was more for alliteration than an apt description of the vehicles. There even was a Fiat Spider but in a sporty red rather than the more sedate gray of the department head's car.

The 10-year-old red Spider had a window paper that listed several restoration and maintenance investments made within the past year that tallied $1,600, which coincidentally was also the seller's asking price. After meeting with the seller, driving the car, and confirming that receipts retained from recent services added to $1,600, we haggled briefly over price before agreeing to $1,400 cash. He seemed content with the deal, while I figured that he had given me a free car and $200 to pay for a year's worth of minor restoration work. In the months to come, I learned the error of my assumptions. Rather than those $1,600 in receipts indicating insurance against any immediate future outlays, they indicated an impending black hole of time and money for anyone trying to keep the car in roadworthy condition. I learned too late why those in the know dubbed a Fiat vehicle a Fix It Again Tomorrow.

## LEADERSHIP LESSON 9.C.
## THINK AHEAD TO MAKE THE
## MOST OF A GIVEN SITUATION.

When I took possession of the Spider, the vinyl rear window was an opaque, amberish color from the harsh UV rays of the Oahu sun. After a few opening and closing cycles of the convertible top, the weathered vinyl proved too brittle to fold and cracked horizontally across the width of the whole car. The daily afternoon rain showers doused the rear seat through the growing window chasm, and the road noise became deafening anytime I drove above 25 mph as the wind worked to further remove the flapping embrittled plastic fragments.

The first time the Spider left me stranded was on a grocery run. The drive to the store was uneventful; the car started without incident and drove as expected all the way into the parking space. I switched off the ignition and hopped out, pocketing the key. After returning minutes later with bags of purchased dairy products and other perishables, I got back in the car, but now it refused to start. From the sound of things, the culprit was the starter motor. After many failed attempts to start the engine and increasingly concerned that my once-cold groceries were quickly baking in the sun, I was able to flag down a couple of Good Samaritans who gamely provided a nice push sufficient for me to compression start the engine by popping the clutch in second gear. Hurray for a manual transmission!

After returning home with my now lukewarm groceries, I was able to properly troubleshoot the problem and confirm the starter motor had an intermittent failure. Research into a replacement indicated a new starter could be had for the same price I had paid for my first used car. Hmm. That was not going to happen anytime soon. The nice thing about Oahu and the Hawaiian Islands in general in a situation such as this is the volcanic origin of the land mass. The island is really a mountain top jutting from the depths of the ocean. There are few areas of level ground aside from the perimeter beaches, and my rental house driveway was nearly as steep as the price of an Italian starter motor. A brief coast down the hill to build momentum and a quick pop of the clutch would serve to start the engine when departing. With a bit of strategic planning before parking the car during outings, I found there was almost always a nearby incline that would provide the needed momentum for a compression start of the engine for the return trip. A starter replacement investment could be deferred.

## LEADERSHIP LESSON 9.D.
## REFRAME "PROBLEMS" AS
## PUZZLES TO BE SOLVED.

The next significant stranding by the Fiat happened while on a date. We were driving to a restaurant for dinner when the car began to lose power. Despite a full tank of gas, the engine acted as though it was running on empty and gave one last gasp before dying. After a few roadside attempts to restart on the intermittent starter, the engine fired up and allowed halting progress toward the restaurant. The evening was ruined by the unreliable ride, but at least the car provided another interesting problem to solve. Troubleshooting this time showed the electric fuel pump to be the issue, a replacement that would cost about 25 percent of the amount I'd paid for the car. That also fell into the not-going-to-happen category, so I removed the pump, disassembled it, cleaned all electrical and mechanical parts, rebuilt it, and reinstalled it. The Spider again ran just fine. That rebuild lasted several months. The second rebuild of the fuel pump lasted just one month. The third lasted a few weeks. When the third rebuild died, I did what needed to be done.

I biked over to the base auto parts store to buy a new electric fuel pump. "Aloha! How can I help you today?" the clerk behind the desk greeted.

"Hello, I'd like to buy an electric fuel pump," I replied with as much hopeful enthusiasm as possible.

"Sure! What year, make, and model is your car?" he eagerly inquired.

"The least expensive electric fuel pump you have in stock will be fine," was my honest answer.

"What?" The clerk gave a look that indicated he had understood my answer but did not know what to make of it.

"I'd like to buy the least expensive electric fuel pump you have in stock," I repeated.

Still incredulous at the ask, the clerk attempted to educate me. "I need to know the year, make, and model of the car to sell you a fuel pump—they're all different."

"I understand that," I assured him. "I'd like to buy the least expensive one you have in stock."

His eager demeanor now gone, the clerk flatly said, "Not just any pump will fit. They are different sizes, different flow rates, different electrical connections, fuel line connections—"

"I understand all that and I'll deal with the installation and making it all work. Can you tell me what pumps you carry?" I again asked.

"I . . . I can't sell you just any pump," he stammered.

"Can you see your inventory by price?" I asked in an effort to overcome the impasse.

"Yes, but I don't see how that matters." He remained skeptical of my request.

"Can you please tell me what car the lowest-priced electric fuel pump you have in stock will fit?" I tried, although his facial expression suggested he still was not following me.

"Um. It looks like the Vega pump is the lowest pri—" he began before I cut him off.

"I'd like to buy a pump for a Chevy Vega."

Mahalo! After much back and forth, the clerk finally agreed to sell me a pump priced at $30. Of course it was not going to fit as a drop-in replacement, so I also bought a few dollars' worth of fuel hose and hose clamps to help with configuring it to my needs and to enable the adaptation of standard fittings to metric. The Fiat original pump nestled in a small well in the trunk, which was where I placed the adapting hoses. The pump itself, which was much larger than the original, I mounted a few inches away. The electrical connections were a trivial puzzle to solve relative to other electrical engineering problems I'd encountered in my studies. I never had another fuel pump issue with the Spider following the transplant.

## LEADERSHIP LESSON 9.E.
## SOMETIMES "SHIT HAPPENS."

While traversing the Likelike Highway during a winter downpour, I observed the Spider's ragtop to be nearly as effective at blocking rain drops as it was wind and road noise. The angry torrents of rain impinging the roof turned into a fine mist as they passed through the top's fabric and saturated the car's interior, myself included. Turning on the defroster in an effort to clear the windshield brought the overall interior climate to that of a steam bath. The humidity was uncomfortable, but the stench was downright nauseating. The plush genuine sheepskin covers that the prior owner had ostensibly installed as a more comfortable alternative to the bare vinyl seats in the Hawaiian sun now put forth the odor of a wet dog lying on the hearth before a toasty fire. The drive in the rain lasted one evening; the stench of the soaked sheepskin seat covers drying in Oahu's heat and humidity lasted for weeks. Removing the seat covers both to eliminate the funk from the car and to expedite the drying process revealed that the seat vinyl had gaping cracks from the car's years sitting in the tropical sun. Could it be that the seller had installed the sheepskin covers more to hide the underlying vinyl condition than to prevent the discomfort of sticking to the seats as he had claimed during the sell?

My family has a peculiar sense of humor. When my sister happened across a white bumper sticker with red lettering that proclaimed "Shit Happens," she thought it just had to adorn my Spider's rear. Given my history with the car, I neatly affixed that sticker to the chrome bar of the rear bumper and forgot about it. While groggily motoring home on the Kamehameha Highway one Sunday morning following a 24-hour Saturday duty shift, my adrenaline spiked as the engine suddenly emitted a deafening roar. Sparks shot into view in in the rearview mirror, and a dead-raising, metal-on-pavement banging came from under the vehicle. When I pulled to the shoulder and looked under the car, the problem became obvious: the muffler had broken loose and was dragging on the pavement. A frantic search of the interior and trunk provided only a single wire clothes hanger from which to fashion a makeshift muffler mount. Still clad in khaki uniform, I wiggled under the car and suffered only mild burns from the muffler and exhaust pipe while bending the clothes hanger into a suitable configuration to hold the muffler more or less in place, or at least to suspend it above the roadway. Relieved to have found a solution, I grabbed up to the rear bumper for leverage to help pull myself from under the car. As I raised my head, there staring me directly in the face between my hands were the words "Shit Happens." Indeed, sometimes it does.

## LEADERSHIP LESSON 9.F.
## COMMUNICATE INTENTIONS
## BEFORE TAKING ACTION.

One fine day in paradise, a JO buddy and I happened to both find ourselves on a rare off-duty weekend day and decided we would tour the island. My car would serve as transportation, as we intended to hit a beach or two and I was much less concerned with the thought of a bit of sand in the old Spider than was he with his shiny, late-model ride. He drove to my house in Aiea and, after loading the Fiat with our needs for the day, we experienced a typical episode of starter motor intermittency. Swinging open the driver's door to give the car a quick shove backward with my left leg out of the level garage and onto the incline of the driveway had become so habitual that I gave it no thought. With the transmission in neutral, I would simply return my left foot to the clutch pedal, close the driver's door, shift into reverse, then release the clutch pedal to compression start the engine as the car gained momentum rolling backward down the driveway. To my buddy in the passenger seat, the failed starter situation seemed to call for his help, and he opened his door with the intention of jumping to the front of the car to give the shove I was already providing with my left leg while comfortably positioned in the driver's seat. The result of our independent actions with lack of communication was the open passenger door gouging an impressive arc from the sheetrock of the garage wall. The impact also rippled the passenger-side quarter panel and buggered the Spider's door hinge alignment.

The bodywork quote to repair the hinge and remove the crease exceeded the blue book value of the car. I opted to adjust the hinges to a serviceable alignment, to ignore the cosmetic customization added that day, and to patch the garage drywall.

At the end of my Pearl Harbor tour of duty, I parked the Fiat Spider 124 back on the Hickam AFB Lemon Lot with a window paper that truthfully disclosed what the buyer would be purchasing for $1,200.

Would it surprise you to know it sold in mere days? Three years of driving for a $200 principal reduction, not to mention the myriad puzzles it presented for me to solve, seemed like a great deal. From speaking with other Fiat owners, I concluded that mine was not so much a lemon as a *cedro*, or *citron*, if you prefer.

## LEADERSHIP LESSONS:

**9.A.** Leverage existing business assets to boost team morale. Many times, leaders will forego solutions or projects that have tremendous potential to boost employee morale due to a mistaken belief that such efforts will cost too much. That is often not the case, especially when leveraging existing assets. The lemon lot is a fine example of an existing asset put to use for employee benefit with virtually no incremental cost.

**9.B.** Be honest in your dealings with others. The seller of the Fiat did not lie, per se. He told the truth, just not the whole truth. I likely would have purchased the car even if he had given full disclosure to the impending maintenance needs. The difference would have been my ongoing pleasure with having done business with him rather than thinking him a bit of a con artist.

**9.C.** Think ahead to make the most of a given situation. The Fiat's starter failure at first seemed a surprise expense that would take an immediate bite from my savings. With a little thinking on the overall situation, however, a better alternative came to mind. By strategically parking on a decline whenever possible, I was able to plan and budget for the starter replacement. I also came to realize that the expense of a new starter would be unnecessary. Why put a brand-new starter on a 10-year-old automobile? Every other piece of the car was used, so it seemed a used starter would be a better match. And it substantially reduced the cost.

The months of deferred repair work while parking on hills also had a comical benefit. When people saw me rolling the car for a compression start, it certainly was a conversation starter!

**9.D.** Reframe "problems" as puzzles to be solved. Dealing with problems is unpleasant. Solving puzzles is fun. Leverage prior experience and knowledge to extend them into creative new solutions. The mental attitude when approaching a given situation will have a tremendous impact on the outcome.

**9.E.** Sometimes "shit happens." Good things do too. It's how you play the cards you are dealt that determines your outlook and success. And in many cases, a sense of humor will reduce the magnitude of any bad happenings.

**9.F.** Communicate intentions before taking action. Had I explained to my friend how I intended to solve the car's nonstart situation, he would have felt no need to attempt to help. Similarly, had he stated how he intended to help, I could have saved him the trouble. Either or both of us stating intentions before acting would have avoided the damage done to the car and the garage.

# 10

# WESTERN PACIFIC
# DEPLOYMENT

## LEADERSHIP LESSON 10.A.
## DEPLOY HUMAN RESOURCE TALENT
## WITH MINDFUL BALANCE.

From the television and magazine ads to the outreach pieces in the campus tribune and the interactions with a recruiter, the Navy sets the expectation that those joining the force will serve at sea. For many recruits, it is the allure of the open water that compels them to enlist. To the typical sailor, deployment at sea is the standard work situation. The underway routine of the seafaring ship is the normal condition; operational watchstanding and functional drills and exercises are the expected work activities and environment.

To those relegated to shipyard duty, however, a ride at sea is considered a privilege. Not only does sea service offer a welcome change to the industrial work in the shipyard, but it is impossible to complete the required professional qualifications without demonstrating proficiency at the actual shipboard watch stations while underway at sea. Without a temporary duty assignment on a seagoing ship, the shipyard-bound officer will fall behind in his career relative to his seagoing peers. For these reasons, the yard-bound ship's wardroom members each anxiously awaited their turn to ride a seagoing sister ship from the fleet.

Watching the slightly more tenured junior officers receive their temporary assignments and deploy on other ships, and then upon their return seeing them receive their dolphins—the submarine force's insignia of professional qualification—provided the needed incentive to keep us toiling away at the unanticipated shipyard duty. Each officer within our wardroom received his turn at sea, his eagerly sought reward and reprieve from the shipyard, based on his relative seniority. This priority system was too logical, fair, and just to question—until it was Mr. Spiro's turn for a sea ride in the relative-seniority rotation.

Mr. Spiro had been found ineligible for submarine sea duty due to a lung condition that developed after he had signed on with the submarine service program. The needs of the Navy determined that he should continue to serve in his submarine overhaul capacity rather than be reassigned to a surface ship where he might continue a viable career. In essence, his career had been served a death sentence since he would never be able to complete his submarine qualifications while being limited to service only in the shipyard. All JOs of the wardroom felt Mr. Spiro's pain.

When what should have been Mr. Spiro's turn for a sea ride arose, something interesting happened. Rather than skipping over Mr. Spiro and assigning the ride to the next most tenured officer, as the junior officers expected, the command instead decided to send the least productive member of the wardroom. Our ship was in the midst of important nuclear reactor plant and engine room upgrades and testing, and rather than pull a fully qualified watch officer (myself) from the shipyard duty rotation, a newer, less qualified officer who had been the subject of several NRRO negative findings instead received the sea assignment reward.

Mr. Spiro's misfortune apparently caused the command to reevaluate the sea ride program and to determine that temporary sea assignment to other ships should no longer be a seniority-based entitlement. The break in the rotation order provided the opportunity to enact a new strategy on sea assignments. They decided to place the needs of our shipyard-bound command before the career aspirations of the officers. And to ensure the needed overhaul work would progress as productively as possible, the least productive members of the wardroom would be the ones selected to participate in the sea rides as they became available.

## LEADERSHIP LESSON 10.B.
## THINK STRATEGICALLY.

The unwritten, unspoken new strategy was much more directed than the prior tenure-based approach. Rather than awaiting notification from another command of a sea ride opportunity and then sending the next most-tenured officer in succession on that temporary assignment, strategic planning was involved. No longer would the command simply react when an opening on another ship presented itself. The inferred new practice was to look ahead to technically challenging events coming up on the shipyard overhaul schedule and to strategically determine who from the wardroom should be present to best clear the technical hurdles, and who could be spared from the duty roster to bring the most value in absentia at that time. Given a little proactive planning and scheduling luck with the seagoing ships, the officer most likely to embarrass himself under the watchful eye of an in-port auditing agency could just so happen to be unavailable for testing and evaluation due to his temporary assignment to another command. Conversely, the most valued players within the wardroom lineup could be denied a seagoing opportunity should the timing conflict with a scheduled command evaluation. This shrewd strategy boosted the command's evaluation scores in the short term (i.e., it made the boss look good) but at a substantial cost to crew morale.

## LEADERSHIP LESSON 10.C.
## POLICIES FORM THE FOUNDATION
## OF THE WORK CULTURE.

In an effort to maximize performance records, the command unwittingly implemented a perverse reward system. The officer whose performance rose above that of his peer group received doubly negative recognition; he had to deal with additional graded examinations under the scrutiny of external auditors, and postponement of career-enhancing sea experience. Meanwhile, the officer whose performance and productivity fell below that of the team at large received doubly positive incentive; he was rewarded with additional career-advancing sea experience, and the luxury of foregoing the dreaded command evaluations. Despite short-term results in the form of higher command test scores, in time, the overall performance of the command began to drift toward mediocrity, as one might expect given the reverse reward incentive structure.

## LEADERSHIP LESSON 10.D.
## GIVE STAR PLAYERS THE
## OPPORTUNITY TO SHINE.

My long-overdue turn for a sea ride finally arrived, and it was a gem. The assigned ship, USS *Buffalo*, had received orders for a six-month Western Pacific tour of duty. The WestPac tour was the most coveted assignment in all the Pacific Fleet. Not only could a WestPac tour represent a meaningful assignment in protecting surface ships of the Pacific Fleet and portions of the west coast of the country during the Cold War period, it also meant a chance to see various foreign ports along the western side of the Pacific Ocean.

From the first night of the guest ride, I was made to feel something of a celebrity. As is customary before a vessel's deployment, the XO of the seabound ship mustered the crew at the dock for a briefing of the tour just prior to getting underway. As the sun fell below the Hawaii horizon, he shared with the crew the plans for the first leg of our journey and concluded by introducing me to the crew, even going so far as to say what a privilege it was for them to have me aboard. Any thought of keeping a low profile and learning seafaring operations by quietly observing the experienced crew dissipated in an instant. I would have to strive to perform to the high expectations now set.

The hosting crew wasted no time in answering the call of duty. In professional fashion, the crew members boarded the ship, took up their assigned watch stations, and made ready to get underway. As the ship pulled away from the pier, I was stationed under instruction with the chief of the watch (CoW) at the dive control panel located in the conning room. The conning area of the ship ("the Conn") is the functional equivalent of an aircraft cockpit. Replete with dials, gauges, lights, levers, and communications gear, it is the command center—the very nerve center—for overall submarine operations. The role of the CoW is to control the submarine's buoyancy and ballast by pumping water into and out of the ship's various tanks as needed for optimal operations, surfaced or submerged, and to raise the submarine's masts and antennas as ordered.

In what to the first-timer seemed a compressed period of orders, reports, and choreographed frenzy, we had reached open water.

"Submerge the ship," the officer of the deck (OOD) ordered.

"Submerge the ship, aye, sir," I affirmed as adrenaline flowed and I twice sounded the dive alarm (think of the klaxon horn's "oogah" sound from old Hollywood movies), announced "Dive! Dive!" over the 1MC to alert the crew, and flipped the valve control switches to vent the fore and aft main ballast tanks of air to submerge the ship.

"Venting forward," reported the OOD as he observed via periscope the spray of seawater from the vent openings on the forward deck. "Venting aft," he called seconds later after pivoting 180 degrees with the scope to confirm the vent fonts on the aft deck. Confirmation of main ballast tank (MBT) valve position is vital to submarine operations. Should an MBT fail to open during submergence, for example, the ship could flounder at a life-threatening angle. Should an MBT valve fail to seal closed when attempting to surface again, the ship would be unable to rest above water.

A ship with a faulty MBT valve is much like a SCUBA diver with a leaky buoyancy compensator.

Within minutes of the order to submerge the ship, we were in our submarine element and I was busily checking the accuracy of prior preparatory work and dockside ballast calculations in readying for this submergence. Errors in fore-aft or port-starboard loading, both of material supplies and in the compensating ballast tank levels, could have serious implications on the ship's handling characteristics and desired state of neutral buoyancy. By the end of the first watch, I had collected an array of qualification signatures for performing tasks that physically were not possible in a shipyard dry dock environment.

As the six-hour watch shifts tallied into days, the host crew remained very accommodating, reviewing my qualification records for still-needed events and scheduling me at watch stations where I could conduct the myriad tasks required to complete my qualification in submarine warfare. As I ascended the qual-status ladder and earned qualifications to stand the various watches, the relationship became mutually beneficial. The crew enjoyed the luxury of having me as an additional watchstander for their duty rotations, and I continued to perform required tasks to gain experience and collect the confirming signatures needed to advance my overall submarine qualification status. The *Buffalo* crew was so in tune to my qualification needs that they would even roust me from the rack if there was a qualification-required evolution to occur when I was not already standing watch. They were clearly invested in my progress and wanted to see me succeed.

## LEADERSHIP LESSON 10.E.
## PUT SAFETY AS THE HIGHEST PRIORITY AT ALL TIMES.

Life onboard a submarine in the open ocean requires notable discipline. To leverage the submarine's most important attribute—the element of surprise—requires constant vigilance toward silence. Utmost care is taken to ensure that equipment and the ship itself is as noise-free as possible, and each individual crew member is also attuned to speak and move as quietly as possible. To prevent any possible noise from footfalls, the hard-heeled, black-leather shoes of shore duty are replaced with one's choice of sneakers. When moving between compartments, the hatches are attentively opened and closed. Even the door to the stall in the head (restroom) is gently secured to ensure no inadvertent bump when closing and latching.

When sufficient qualified watchstanders were available, the watch schedule for a given station operated in a relatively luxurious three-shift rotation. On a six-hour watch cadence, this allowed for 12 hours off for every six hours on watch. Given the absence of daylight undersea (there were neither portholes nor sun to shine through them at depth), the submarine can ignore the 24-hour day/night cycle of land-dwelling life and operate on its own 18-hour day. A typical cycle might be to stand watch for six hours, spend an hour completing a report of the watch just stood, take the next five hours to study additional qualification exam materials, and solicit "checkouts" on the material (asking a qualified watchstander to confirm demonstration of content knowledge in a manner consistent with qualification procedures during reactor prototype training), maybe catch a quick meal, then grab four hours of sleep before rising and touring the next watch station before relieving the offgoing watchstander. Thus completes the 18-hour cycle while starting the next.

Note there is no mention of showering in the typical daily cycle. One must drink, one must eat, one must carry one's load for the collective good (stand watch, study, and qualify to stand additional watch duty stations), and one might consider sleeping (though it's not absolutely required). Showering is optional, however, not just in the interest of Maslow's hierarchy of human priorities, but also in the interest of water conservation. Drinking water, and water to sustain proper operation of the ship's equipment are higher on the priority list than a quick shower, which can be had every two or three days.

The ship's internal lighting condition is the one reliable indicator of actual 24-hour day/night cycles in the world outside the ship. The officers qualified to stand watch as the officer of the deck pay keen attention to the ship's location and to local sunrise and sunset times.

Should there be a need to bring the ship up to periscope depth to have a look around, the OOD must readily be able to see in the external lighting conditions. During times of external daylight, the submarine's interior is well lit in the manner of most work environments. Past sunset in the ship's present location, the ship is "Rigged for Red," a configuration in which most lights are extinguished save for red lamps that dimly color the passageways and working surfaces. Working in red-lit conditions allows for immediate visibility by the OOD when observing the world via periscope at night. The inconvenience to the crew working under red lights is minor relative to the safety advantage afforded to all by having the OOD's vision adapted to night vision.

## LEADERSHIP LESSON 10.F.
## LEVERAGE 5S+1 TECHNIQUES.

When there are too few qualified watchstanders available to support a three-shift rotation, the two-shift duty schedule put in place is colloquially known as "Port and Starboard." This six-hours-on, six-hours-off cycle can rapidly wear down any crew. When working a two-shift duty cycle, it is necessary to make tough choices on how to invest the precious time not standing watch. Remember that the first hour off duty is spent completing the watch report, and the last hour prior to relieving the watch is spent touring the plant and readying to competently relieve the watch. How to spend those precious four interim hours? Maybe grab a bite to eat? Try to squeeze in a quick qualification checkout? Hit the rack for a sleep period measured in minutes? When was the last shower? The two-shift duty cycle is also known crassly as "port and stupid," or sometimes as "port and report."

The days at sea were anything but routine. The "typical" cycles described were interrupted regularly to run training drills. Drills to simulate various reactor plant emergencies and to ensure war-fighting readiness were frequent. "Field Day" also took place every Saturday, in which every crew member did his part to clean the ship from top to bottom, fore to aft, and side to side. There was no sleeping during Field Day; every person on board was up and participating in the activity to ensure clean, uncluttered access to every inch of the vessel. Maintaining gear and equipment "stowed for sea" is imperative. Having a place for everything and everything in its place not only ensures that a given item is readily available in a known location when needed, it also prevents the risk of damage or injury from falling or flying objects when the ship experiences a steep angle or roll.

## LEADERSHIP LESSON 10.G.
## PLAN AND CARE FOR THE NEW RECRUIT.

During my three-month ride on the ship's scheduled six-month deployment, I essentially completed my qualification book for submarine operations. The hosting wardroom and crew had fully integrated me as one of their own. From the welcoming all-hands introduction upon my arrival, to giving overt attention to my qualifications progress and rapidly including me on watchstanding rosters throughout my time on board, they included me in all activities as a valued member of their crew. Appreciating the extensive knowledge of a ship's equipment and systems I had gained during shipyard overhaul activities, the host ship scheduled me as an engineering instructor and mentor during my time with them. In a truly synergistic relationship, I learned from the crew the ways of seafaring operations while they in return learned from me the inner workings of the ship's equipment.

# LEADERSHIP LESSONS:

**10.A.** Deploy human resource talent with mindful balance. It is the manager's role to leverage human resource talent in a manner that will advance the collective cause. It is the leader's role to keep a careful eye on the balance between what's in it for the company and what's in it for the individual. The win-win between these two interests must be apparent at all times if the leader is to maintain the respect of the team and high workforce morale.

When Mr. Spiro became ineligible for sea duty, the leadership missed the opportunity to show empathy for his situation and made matters worse by compromising overall morale by changing the reward structure without proactively informing the affected team.

**10.B.** Think strategically. Give some time and thought not only to analyze potential business actions, but also to consider the perspectives of valued employees. Anticipate what others will likely do in response to your leadership decisions and actions. And whenever possible, seek input from team members before effecting changes that will impact them.

**10.C.** Policies form the foundation of the work culture. Think, think again, then think a third time before implementing or changing a policy. Ask yourself, what could go wrong with a policy? How could it impact morale or motivate workers toward undesirable outcomes? This critical thinking before changing any policy is essential for identifying and mitigating potential unintended consequences.

**10.D.** Give star players the opportunity to shine. Yes, give them the most challenging and visible assignments. No, do not toss every last task that comes along their way. Beware the natural tendency to (unwittingly) load the star player with so much work that performance falls to the norm.

**10.E.** Put safety as the highest priority at all times. Walk the talk. Your crew watches your feet more closely than they do your mouth. For this reason, you should demonstrate safety as top priority in actions as well as words. This lesson is so important that it bears repeating.

**10.F.** Leverage 5S+1 techniques. Doing so will both improve efficiency and create a safe work environment. 5S is a well-proven Japanese methodology that results in a workplace that is clean, uncluttered, and well organized to help reduce waste and optimize productivity.

For those who are unfamiliar with 5S, the key aspects of the method include:

- *Seiri*: To separate needed tools, parts, and instructions from unneeded materials and to remove the unneeded ones from the workplace.
- *Seiton*: To neatly arrange and identify materials and tools for ease of use.
- *Seiso*: To conduct a cleanup campaign.
- *Seiketsu*: To conduct *seiri*, *seiton*, and *seiso* on an ongoing basis to maintain a workplace in proud condition.
- *Shitsuke*: To form the habit of always following the first four directives.

As time progressed, experience suggested the benefit to adding a sixth S, for Safety. This is written as 5S+1 or sometimes as 6S, to ensure that safety retains a place in the forefront of everyone's mind at all times. The Navy generally refers to this as "ship shape," having a place for everything and keeping everything in its place when not in use. I found 5S+ 1 to be an effective approach to bringing safety and efficient housekeeping to front of mind for lab and factory workers.

**10.G.** Plan and care for the new recruit. Giving attention to a new recruit even before his or her arrival will build morale and help to form a positive image of the team. A hearty welcome and introduction upon joining the workforce will set the tone for the recruit's success with your team. (See also leadership lesson 15.a.)

# 11

# PORTS OF CALL

## LEADERSHIP LESSON 11.A.
## APPRECIATE DIVERSITY.

One feature of the Navy recruiter's advertising that was unassailably true was the promise of seeing the world. After the first two months of undersea duty during our Western Pacific deployment, we made a port call at Subic Bay in the Philippine Islands to replenish supplies.

While the nuclear-powered ship could travel the world many times over before needing to refuel, the same could not be said for the crew. We were anxious to bring on fresh produce and to refill the depleting refrigerator and freezer racks. Fresh lubricating oil for the engine room machinery was also on the preventive maintenance schedule.

In preparation before the shore visit, the XO mustered the crew for a briefing on our stay. He ensured that we were aware of our planned duration in port and the key deliverables we must accomplish aboard ship. For those fortunate enough to have earned time off the ship with a liberty call, the XO ensured that crew members understood local customs and expectations by overviewing key details about our host country before anyone disembarked. After sharing a few details of interest on local climate, employment, and per capita income, he cautioned that among the local norms was that it is a punishable offense to insult someone. Anyone intending to exit the base and to visit the Olongapo surrounds was to remain aware at all times of the need to avoid any potential upset or insult to the local population.

After observing and helping to load the stores and provisions, and standing watch on the first two days in port, a couple of the wardroom JOs with time for liberty invited me to join them for a trip to see some local sites. The first observation of note was the putrid river separating the base from the town. The stench was overpowering as we walked across the bridge above the disgusting flow. The substance slowly moving toward the bay was raw sewage, earning this stream the colloquial designation "Shit River."

As we made our way into town along Magsaysay Drive, the colorful shops brought to mind photographs from an earlier time. The shops' proprietors were doing what they could with the resources they had to add value to the local community. There were stores with every sort of item for sale, some with indoor space to browse and some set up flea market–style along the walkway. Street vendors offered local food items, some selling assorted fruit pieces and some selling what appeared to be geckos and chicken feet on bamboo skewers cooked over bits of charcoal.

## LEADERSHIP LESSON 11.B.
## ADMIRE CREATIVITY.

We paused at various shops and stands along the way. In one fascinating nook we witnessed a skilled metalworker hunched over what looked to be an aged section from a tree stump, tapping away on what could have been a carpenter's nail with a rock for a hammer. With such crude tools he was fashioning truly impressive pieces of metal art. On display he had bright metalwork items etched with various scenes and lettering, in combinations of silver and gold. Several of us purchased custom belt buckles hand worked to our specifications. Mine were two-tone silver and gold with renditions of my duty submarine and its name and hull number, complete with my name. He asked $5 total for the two buckles, on par with the price of plain, standard-issue USN brass buckles for the uniform web belts. The base metal he used in the buckles was unknown, but the finished product appeared to be chrome on the silver-colored areas and polished brass on the yellow-gold areas. It was astonishing what the man could tap-etch into metal using only such basic tools and skilled discipline.

## LEADERSHIP LESSON 11.C.
## TRAVEL THE WORLD BUT LEAVE IGNORANCE BEHIND.

One clothing store we browsed had an impressive selection of brightly colored, polo-style shirts. Although the shirt labels read Ralph Lauren Polo, the fabric knit felt to be of lesser quality and the embroidered polo player with mallet astride a horse was rendered a bit askew on the chest. The asking price was also some 85 percent below what a genuine article would command stateside. After considering the offerings for a few minutes, we decided to move along for the time being without making a purchase. As we stepped from the store onto the walkway, a teenage boy followed and slung a polo shirt over the shoulder of one in our party. Startled, my buddy asked, "What are you doing?"

"Giving you a shirt," said the boy.

"It's not mine," replied my bewildered buddy, lifting the shirt from his shoulder and handing it back to the boy.

"You refuse my gift?" persisted the boy.

"I'm not buying it."

"You refuse my gift. You are insulting me. You should accept it and give me something in return."

"No, I'm not insulting you," said my now-concerned buddy.

Our minds were collectively racing as we understood the unfolding scheme. "Tell you what," he continued, "I accept your gift, and I give you in return this shirt."

"You are refusing my gift. You are insulting me!" protested the boy.

"I accepted your gift. Now here is my gift to you," stated my buddy as he handed the shirt back to the boy. "If you do not accept it, you are insulting ME!" he closed and rapidly walked away.

I had the misfortune of being a few steps behind our party when this action unfolded. The puzzled youth looked at me, dejectedly holding the proffered shirt. It was apparent that he had already lived a hard life. His teeth were jagged, his joints knobby, and his frame gaunt. As I moved forward to rejoin my party, the afflicted youth grabbed and sank his teeth into my left forearm. As I reflexively pulled away, I was mindful to shove with an open right hand rather than to strike with closed fist, which I may well have done without the XO's prior words of caution. Free of the scene, I was happy to note there were only bruised toothmarks and saliva on my arm; he had not broken the skin. We decided there had been enough excitement for one outing and headed back to base.

## LEADERSHIP LESSON 11.D.
## UNDERSTAND CONTEXT.

If the harsh environment of the river crossing was not enough to elicit a gag reflex as we had made our way into town, the realization on the return trip certainly triggered a reaction. There were skinny local boys, perhaps eight to 14 years of age, eagerly waiting below the bridge for those crossing to toss in coins that they could dive to retrieve from the murky liquid. It seemed surreal that these kids were actually diving into the filth, and having to open their eyes in raw sewage below the surface, to grab a few pesos or cents.

## LEADERSHIP LESSON 11.E.
## SPEAK UP.

I inquired with one of the crew members happily tossing coins over the bridge rail the reason for his actions. A bit intoxicated from his trip into town, he remarked that he was helping the kids and their families who needed the money more than he. The fact that the kids were waiting for tossed coins indicated this to be a known and expected practice, he noted. I suggested that if the coin tossers truly wanted to help the local children they could simply hand money to them, and perhaps in paper denominations rather than pocket change. The excitement and laughter stopped as those enjoying the spectacle considered my unpopular words.

## LEADERSHIP LESSON 11.F.
## MAINTAIN PERSPECTIVE.

Back on base, rather than returning directly to the submarine, we went to an officer's reserved area to relax. It was a small but functional building with a kitchen space, room to watch television, and sleeping quarters. San Miguel beer, the local libation, was a veritable bargain at $0.90 for a six-pack. Where else can you buy a six-pack of beer and leave a respectable tip all for a single US greenback?

Some of the other crew members brought back stories of sites, bars, and restaurants farther out than we had traveled on foot. They suggested we catch a jeepney ride to reach these destinations. A jeepney?

A jeepney began life as a four-wheel drive, olive drab, ubiquitous US military vehicle left behind after World War II. The industrious Filipino population found a use for the many surplus US Willys Jeeps by converting them for civilian transportation. They lengthened the original American vehicle to accommodate more passengers, fashioned a roof to ward off the scorching Philippine sun, and on some mods even removed the seats and installed two benches that stretched lengthwise on either side with a narrow aisle in between to allow more seating space. Jeepney drivers personalized their remade vehicles with vivid colors and images of anything that suited their fancy. A jeepney ride was both practical and an experience not to be missed.

The crusty old seafaring shipmates with prior visits to the Philippine Islands under their belts told us the local rates we should expect to pay for jeepney transport to and from various destinations. They warned us to beware the jeepney driver that would try to take advantage of the naive among us. With the conversion value of the Philippine peso equaling only a few US cents, the equivalent value of the fares seemed impossibly low. In most cases the price of the ride would have seemed a reasonable number even if paid in US dollars; when paid in pesos, the price seemed incomprehensible.

As forewarned, a jeepney operator quoted us a rate far higher than the norm, and the haggling began. He lowered the initial quote but refused to come any lower than 25 percent above the rate our seasoned insiders had shared. Momentarily miffed with the feeling that we were literally and figuratively being taken for a ride, I remembered that the peso price gap represented mere pennies in US-dollar terms.

———

Hong Kong harbor was another port visit planned during our WestPac deployment. The sheer number of vessels plying the waterways required that only the most experienced crew members man the controls while piloting the ship to our designated moorage. Small craft and massive ships alike powered through the congestion, adding confounding wakes to the already strong tidal currents.

Given local trepidation with a nuclear-powered vessel in the harbor waters, our designated moorage was distant from shore, alongside and tethered tandem to an anchored surface ship. This arrangement made for an interesting disembarking process of climbing a rope ladder from the deck of the submarine, up the side of the surface ship, walking across the deck of the surface ship, and descending collapsible stairs down the opposite side of the surface ship to an attached floating platform where a small boat was docked to transfer personnel to shore. The configuration made for interesting crossing as the two ships, rope ladder, landing platform, and small boat each bobbed independently as dictated by the waves and winds.

A notable benefit of the ride onboard a submarine relative to that on a surface ship is the calm underway environment. When the seas are rough, a surface ship is tossed about at the mercy of nature. The surface sailor must develop "sea legs" in order to compensate for the swaying footing while standing or walking, and those afflicted by seasickness are well advised to not apply for such duty. While those sailing the ocean's surface are tossed about in a storm, a submarine plows along in serene calm below the swells and wind. This benefit of running deep through calm seas at all times proved to be an indirect liability to submarine sailors on the surface. The bobbing motion of the small transport craft had several of the submariners turning shades of green and feeling queasy before reaching shore.

## LEADERSHIP LESSON 11.G.
## PROTECT THE ENVIRONMENT.

Adding further insult to the seasick travelers was the ambient funk of the harbor. When the Hong Kong—or "fragrant harbor"—name was originally applied, the aroma was likely that of local plants gently wafting across fresh sea breezes. On the night of our arrival, the air was indeed fragrant, but with the stench of human activity befouling the environment. The reek in the air by itself would have caused queasiness. When combined with the motion sickness, several of the passengers had an altogether discomforting start to our brief stay.

## LEADERSHIP LESSON 11.1.
## BUY DIRECT.

Happily on solid ground, our landing party delighted in the local cuisine and colorful lights and signage along the avenues. One among us who had visited Hong Kong previously led an outing to the clothing district where bargains could be found on wardrobe upgrades. Several of us also purchased custom tailored suits of fine European wools. Selecting the fabric, style, and desired cut for a custom-fit suit was an adventure for those of us whose only civilian suit was the cringeworthy polyester selection worn years ago during the nuclear power program interviews in D.C. The tailors were able to take initial measurements and move to fittings and final alterations within 48 hours in an amazing display of artisan skill.

While we were strolling along and taking in the sights, a gentleman approached and inquired our interest in purchasing a Rolex watch. The roving salesman carried several impressive imposters on his person, offering them for USD25 each. The attention to detail was remarkable; the only obvious telltale sign that the articles were not genuine was the stop-motion of the second hand as the quartz movement ticked by the seconds rather than the continual sweep of a true Rolex movement. Several of us bought a watch or two. I fancied them to be intriguing gifts for family and friends back home so asked the salesman if he had others in both men's and women's styles. He seemed to size me up for a moment before indicating that I should follow him from the open street to a side alley.

I had some trepidation in following him. A transaction that seemed a bit sketchy on the street seemed ill-advised if not downright dangerous down a proverbial dark alley. Intrigued by where this might lead, my adrenaline rushed as I cautiously followed him from the bustle of the street to the secluded confines of alleys and vacant corridors inside multiple buildings. After a few minutes, we arrived at a nondescript door, behind which was what would best be described as a cramped closet filled with hundreds of watches. I carefully selected from golds, silvers, and two-tones, with faces of white, blue, red, and green. Some dazzled with faux diamonds; others left the sparkling to highly polished surfaces. Before departing, I purchased one for each family member in a model I believed they would most appreciate. Buying in bulk, I paid USD20 apiece.

## LEADERSHIP LESSON 11.J.
## SET A BUDGET.

This was not the first Hong Kong visit for one member of our party. His tales of fashion bargains had caused his wife to insist upon being included on any return visit. She had flown to meet him during this port call and found the clothing prices simply irresistible. Seeing most every article on the racks priced at mere pennies on the dollar compared to those back home, she felt compelled to buy one of everything. As my sorry colleague noted at the time, "I could go broke saving all this money."

## LEADERSHIP LESSON 11.H.
## WHAT WILL GO WRONG?

At the end of the evening, we made our way back to the submarine by again boarding a small craft, powering a considerable distance over rocking swells back to the anchored surface ship, making our way onto the floating platform as it bobbed alongside the ship with the forces of nature, scaled the retractable ladder up the side of the ship, crossed the topside deck, then descended the rope ladder down the opposite side to again reach our submarine home. Upon descending the ladder below deck on the sub, I came upon the duty officer, who was looking much the worse for wear. I inquired his condition and reason behind his appearance.

It seems the tidal flow and winds in the harbor were even more energetic than they had appeared from our small transit craft. While we were enjoying our visit in the city, the buildings had afforded protection from the strong winds, and we were oblivious to the tidal flow. Out in the harbor, those aboard the submarine had been much more exposed. The force of the currents and winds had overcome the mooring lines, and the submarine had begun to drift apart from the safety of the anchored surface ship. The crew members remaining onboard the sub had an evening of harrowing excitement, working topside during the storm to restrain the sub's movement, tighten the mooring lines, and prevent any further chance of separation from the security of the anchored surface ship.

## LEADERSHIP LESSON 11.K.
## PROTECT INTELLECTUAL PROPERTY.

The faux Rolex watches were a huge hit back home. My brother-in-law had always wanted one but could never justify the price. Even after I explained that it was not genuine, he loved the gift. A year later, when I brought the gold President's Day-Date model watch with screw-down crown and hidden-clasp bracelet I had kept for myself to a jeweler for battery replacement, he was conflicted. The jeweler stated that he should not service this watch due to it being a knockoff but he had never seen the like of its exterior quality and was intrigued to see the internal movement. The tool required to open the case was that of a genuine Rolex. Inside he noted a high-end Japanese quartz movement. He asked where I had gotten the watch, estimating its value at several hundred dollars. I told him I had paid $20 for it in a back alley in Hong Kong.

## LEADERSHIP LESSON 11.L.
## STRETCH.

A brief stop in Busan, South Korea, enabled the crew to experience a few of the local customs. The wardroom participated in an enjoyable outdoor dinner with the main food cooked at the table over hot coals. A gentle breeze brought relief from the humid air while carrying the mouthwatering smell of the delicious barbecue meal. Kimchi was a new experience for several of us that complemented the various protein offerings. Spices used in the pickling process were tasty and induced a flush of perspiration. We learned by observing our local hosts and following the lead of our senior officers. Sharing and savoring were key themes, rather unlike the rushed chow sessions aboard ship where the main purpose was energy replenishment and basic sustenance. Taking time to enjoy the meal and company was a pleasant change. The single drawback to the memorable meal was the leg pain induced by sitting bent at the knees and hips for a prolonged period at the low table.

## LEADERSHIP LESSON 11.M.
## P⁷: PROPER PRIOR PLANNING PREVENTS PISS POOR PERFORMANCE.

An intrepid JO buddy planned to see the local countryside via a self-guided bus tour one afternoon. He had researched bus schedules, fares, and routes, and was planning to spend the day taking in the sights. I had the afternoon off duty and decided to ride along with him rather than to spend the time aboard ship doing yet more studying.

The trip began per plan. We walked to the bus stop, purchased tickets, and timely boarded the bus. The ride was pleasant as we rumbled along, observing the local businesses, homes, and daily life of the local populace. After a while, we decided to disembark at one of the stops and stroll among the street crowds for a more immersive experience. As we walked, we noted a subtle yet distinct change in our sightings. At our point of origin, all signage had been bilingual. Lettering was in both Hangul and English. Where we now found ourselves, all signs were in Hangul; gone was the English. No worries. We remembered the general course of our walk and would simply retrace our steps back to where the bus had dropped us.

Back at the bus stop, we more closely examined the tickets we had purchased. Similar to the local signage, the origin tickets featured both Hangul and English letters. Much to our despair, the return tickets bore only Hangul. We realized the adventure factor of our outing was increasing geometrically as we labored to match the characters, one by one, between tickets and signs. Efforts to speak with local people were fruitless, as their English skills were only marginally better than our Korean. Although we found no perfect match between ticket and bus sign lettering, we found a match close enough that we gamely boarded a passing bus with high hopes of unwinding our trek and returning to base. The bus color scheme differed from the original, but the fact that the bus driver accepted our tickets with no objection gave us some hope.

As we motored along, we were torn between enjoying the new sights and the nagging fear that we may well have boarded the wrong bus. Our intent in taking the trip was to see local sights, but the fact that we were clearly driving somewhere new rather than merely reversing the route of the original bus was a tad disconcerting. About the time we were having serious reservations about our ride, the bus slowed, then stopped in the middle of the road. Before we could understand the reason for the stop, the door swung open and uniformed, armed men entered. Panic might be too strong of a word to describe the situation, but we both were suddenly concerned for what might come next as we quietly suggested between us the possible options. The armed men studied all the passengers intently and spoke briefly and unintelligibly (at least to us) as they made their way up and down the bus aisle. As suddenly as they had boarded, the men seemed satisfied and left. The driver closed the door and resumed driving. Who were they? We never knew for certain. After a bit more driving, the bus regained our confidence as we started to notice familiar sights. Not long after, it dropped us off in proximity to our point of origin. Whew.

———

With our submarine surfaced and cruising into Tokyo Wan (Bay), we gained new confidence in the human race as we watched the myriad proximate seafarers pilot their vessels through the congested ship traffic.

The water traffic was heavy, yet each vessel, regardless of national origin, tucked neatly and logically into the procession of inbound or outbound traffic lanes. It took considerable energy to recognize and track the vessels as they merged with the prevailing traffic flows, but each ship dutifully made their intentions known and maintained safe passage.

Our destination was Yokosuka in Japan's Kanagawa Prefecture. With the submarine safely moored and the duty roster for completion of necessary shore tasks known, my first stop once disembarked was the Fleet Recreation Center. The Fleet Rec Center was a welcome respite after months at sea. The gymnasium proved well appointed, with various hardwood courts for pick-up games, equipment and weights for resistance training, workout clothing for rent or purchase, locker rooms, and showers. Such accommodations would hardly be considered luxuries by the typical high school student within the continental US, but in the eyes of a sailor stepping from the ship amid a months-long deployment, the exercise this gym afforded gave a massive boost to energy and morale.

## LEADERSHIP LESSON 11.N.
## FAMILIES MATTER.

Also in port during our visit was a US aircraft carrier. The enormity of a carrier, a veritable floating city unto itself, is impressive to behold. A temporary battery of telephone booths had been placed dockside near the carrier, allowing the thousands of sailors to place telephone calls to loved ones back home. In an era before cellular mobile phones and ubiquitous internet coverage, the pay phone was the primary communication tool. The lines of sailors awaiting their turn for a few minutes' use of the pay phones left a lasting realization that for every person on the front lines, there is a family support structure behind the scenes.

## LEADERSHIP LESSON 11.0.
## LESS IS MORE.

A visit into town gave us visitors an appreciation for the population density, and the attention given to cleanliness and orderliness. The absence of litter, the disciplined patterns of walk, and the flow of traffic in miniaturized vehicles all attested to the focus on efficient, practical, and harmonious use of space.

Our first stop, FootTown, was a highly recommended destination. Its four stories, built directly under Tokyo Tower, contained fascinating museums, restaurants, and shops. The main attractions were the observation decks of Tokyo Tower high above, which presented visitors with a sweeping view over the city, the bay, and the horizon as far as the eye could see. The elevated platforms offered dizzying heights and astonishing views, especially to a crew that has been living no higher than sea level for months.

## LEADERSHIP LESSONS:

**11.A.** Appreciate diversity. The world is filled with people living their lives in ways different from what you know to be the norm. The diverse customs and traditions may not of themselves be "better" or "worse" than those of your own upbringing, but their difference makes them valuable for provoking new ways of thinking. Study diverse ways of doing things before deciding upon a preferred way for any given situation.

**11.B.** Admire creativity. Artistry and craftsmanship come in all forms. The man who produces impressive and functional pieces of art using only rudimentary tools is a true craftsman. Avoid any thoughts of pity or disdain for his current craft. Think instead of what amazing works he might accomplish with better tools.

**11.C.** Travel the world but leave ignorance behind. Study local customs and laws prior to visiting new places. Learn a few words or key phrases of the local language. Opening yourself up to local ways will only enrich your experience of a foreign place.

**11.D.** Understand context. The child who would dive into raw sewage to collect a peso is doing what is necessary to survive. The person selling chicken feet or skewered lizards cooked over hot coals is demonstrating entrepreneurship with available resources. Resist the knee-jerk reaction to judge, and aim instead to see these situations with a clear understanding of their context.

**11.E.** Speak up. Help others whenever and wherever possible. Do not take advantage of those less fortunate, and have the courage to intervene when encountering those who would. Voicing unpopular truths and making your voice heard can also save everyone time and heartache in the long run. Recall from Chapter 7 the situation when a spike in disqualifications led the CO to lock us in a room until we reached consensus on the root cause of the issue? In that situation, had I more passionately spoken up and made the case for complacency as our issue during the first go-around, all of the wardroom officers might have saved hours locked in that stuffy room.

**11.F.** Maintain perspective. A 25 percent price increase seems a relatively enormous insult. Yet when viewed in the absolute, 25 percent may represent a mere nickel that is not worth any upset.

**11.G.** Protect the environment. Through many decades, the natural fragrance of Hong Kong harbor was transformed to the odor of human activity. Exhaust from automobiles, fumes from the harbor ships, and the inevitable trash from human activity have substantially shifted the area from its wild namesake, as is the case in most any large city.

Understand the environmental impact of potential projects or activities, and ensure the environmental assessment is weighted appropriately in the decision process.

**11.H.** What will go wrong? Before taking action, consider what will go wrong. This mindset of what *will* go wrong is a step deeper into critical thinking than considering what *could* go wrong. By taking this approach, I have many times foreseen potential issues and modified the course of action ahead of time to avoid or minimize a potential mishap.

In the case of the mooring lines, the stormy weather conditions provided ample forewarning that nature would test the tandem anchorage. Special attention to securing additional lines from the onset would have been prudent.

**11.I.** Buy direct. When the opportunity presents itself to shorten the supply chain, purchasing directly from the source is most efficient.

**11.J.** Set a budget. And stick to it. Know your available balance and operate within your means. A corollary rule is to give back to your organization any budgetary amount that goes unspent. Should you be able to complete the scope of a given project for less than the budgeted amount, release the funds back to the organization to put toward the next higher use. Resist the temptation to use project underspend on miscellaneous purchases and the finance team will appreciate your efficient management practices.

**11.K.** Protect intellectual property. When presented with an ersatz watch, my youthful reaction was giddy humor at finding such an impressive replica for such a ridiculously low price. The mature view considers value lost to the company or person whose IP is being exploited for uncompensated gain by others when counterfeit products exchange hands.

**11.L.** Stretch. Most people are aware of the health benefits from physical exercise. Society reminds us of the benefits of a regular fitness regimen and encourages us to remain active. The benefits of stretching muscles and maintaining limber joints are at least as important but less commonly emphasized.

**11.M.** $P^7$: Proper Prior Planning Prevents Piss Poor Performance. The alliteration and crass wording makes $P^7$ a memorable tool to assist in achieving desirable outcomes. In most any undertaking, having a plan is a good idea. In the particular excursion into the South Korean countryside, learning a few common phrases, a few words, or even Hangul characters before venturing forth would have avoided unnecessary angst on the trip.

**11.N.** Families matter. Remember to appreciate and recognize the family support structure behind each worker or employee. A happy and productive employee stems from contentment at home.

**11.O.** Less is more. When space is scarce, smaller is better. When time is of essence, fewer words win out. I will long remember the instructor who said at the end of a class, "I apologize for the lecture being so long; I didn't have time to make it short."

# 12

# CHANGE IN COMMAND

## LEADERSHIP LESSON 12.A.
## ENSURE EVERYONE KNOWS
## WHO HAS AUTHORITY.

A truly fascinating aspect of the Navy's organizational structure is the dynamic rotation of leadership responsibility. Whether brought up through the Naval Academy regimen, Officer Candidate School, or NROTC, the plebes, officer candidates, or cadets learn that leadership positions are both a duty and temporary. In school, there is an assigned leader for each company each day. That designated leader is responsible for mustering classmates, ensuring all are present or accounted for at each planned class or event, and otherwise shepherding their charges while carrying out the plan of the day. A formal exchange of words, "I relieve you" and "I stand relieved," marks the transfer of responsibilities from an offgoing duty officer to the oncoming officer. This transfer of leadership occurs regularly and at all levels, to mark the changes of responsibilities between officers at watch stations, divisions, departments, commands, fleets, and even the entire US Navy.

## LEADERSHIP LESSON 12.B.
## YOUR LEADERSHIP STYLE HAS IMPACT.

The CO of my first assigned ship had the unfortunate habit of inducing anxiety among enlisted personnel and officers alike. His brash, outspoken, opinionated nature made him difficult to endure at times. He almost seemed to enjoy making subordinates nervous, keeping them off balance, and generally intimidating people with his presence. Most of the crew operated in constant fear of triggering another of his outbursts; his temper and penchant for shouting were known all too well. Even "fun" events such as the annual fleet field day, when the crews of the ships in the fleet would picnic together and compete in various activities like tug-of-war, brought out his overly competitive side. Whereas other crews were having fun just showing up and tugging on the rope, our crew was made to practice tug-of-war technique in advance—and suffer berating should we lose a competition. Yet even if we won, it was somehow devoid of true satisfaction or joy; we were just glad to have avoided the boss's verbal disdain.

The CO worked himself into an exasperation trap. The more desperately he willed his crew to outperform, the more frustrated he became at the slightest imperfection in performance and the more shamelessly he would shout words of criticism. All the while, the crew that at one time may have wanted to please him came to operate in a mode of fear that they would disappoint him. And the more the crew feared making an error, the more error prone they became. It was a downward spiral of negative reinforcement: The more exasperated the CO became with the crew's performance, the more he exuded disappointment in them, the further their morale eroded, and the lower their performance descended. The CO was not a bad person; he truly wanted operational excellence. The finer points of leadership such as inspiring subordinates to perform to higher levels and leading by example just did not come easily for him.

## LEADERSHIP LESSON 12.C.
## LEAVE A LEGACY.

A tradition on the eve of a CO's impending departure is for the wardroom to conduct an informal dinner party to celebrate fond memories of the departing CO's tenure leading the command. During this party, the wardroom members bring gag gifts to punctuate various memorable events of the CO's period in command. At the time of the first CO's going-away party, the wardroom officers presented various trinkets deemed likely to bring a chuckle to those in on the joke. Many of the jokes were lost on me, as they evoked memories of events that had occurred prior to my joining the command. I lacked history with the command and had struggled to find a suitable gag gift. The CO and I had not been particularly close and serving in the shipyard under his command had not been the source of many jovial memories. The only gift that came to mind was a large tube of Preparation H. It seemed reasonable that an open-minded interpretation of the marketing claim it "shrinks hemorrhoidal tissue" might infer it would make a flaming asshole go away. I tested my choice of gag gift on a few of the JOs, who grew wide-eyed and gasped. Their laughter seemed a bit nervous and fearful, so I went with the newbie excuse for failing to present a gift.

———

The formal Hail and Farewell ceremony was truly cause for celebration, and optimism was in the air. The new CO was the antithesis of his predecessor. He was an academic, well studied, and humble; he was comfortable with himself. Our new leader brought new life, excitement, and enthusiasm to the command. His quiet-spoken, calm, approachable personality unleashed new potential within the crew virtually overnight. Those who had been withdrawn and solitary under the prior regime now were speaking up and acting more like teammates. And as people opened up, more stories about the outrageous antics of the departed CO came to light. How had the XO tolerated the prior CO, buffering the wardroom and the crew from the wrath of such a boss? Make no mistake, neither the XO nor the new CO encouraged the airing of sea stories about the departed CO, but the catharsis compelled the crew to share.

The transition from one leader to the next was flawless, with no interruption to daily operations and an immediate uptick in crew morale.

During a temporary duty assignment (TDA) to go on a sea ride with another ship, I had the good fortune to experience another change in command. The ship was a top performer, with a capable and motivated crew. The CO-to-be joined us during a Western Pacific deployment to gain firsthand experience with the crew and command assets. During the weeks of his ride-along, the incoming boss toured all spaces of the ship, observing operations and getting to know the crew and the overall command capabilities.

The departing CO was rightfully proud of his crew. He put the ship through its paces, running fast, running deep, running quiet, and at the limits of maneuvering angles, course changes, and depth changes. The incoming CO had already had JO, department head, and XO tours of duty under his belt and had attended pre-CO school to learn all theoretical aspects of commanding a fast attack nuclear submarine. The ride-along trip cemented his years of classroom, lab, and actual experience with specific knowledge of his particular ship and crew.

The crew seemed indifferent to the impending change in command as they performed their daily watchstanding duties. They had enjoyed three years of excellent command performance with the outgoing CO and they understood that, as is the Navy's norm, it was his time to move on to other career opportunities. The incoming CO seemed a capable, engaging candidate to carry on the crew's string of award wins for leading performance. This was a stark contrast to the change in command I had experienced in the shipyard, where the change in leadership personalities and styles was profound.

## LEADERSHIP LESSON 12.0.
## BE MINDFUL OF THE SITUATION.

While stationed in the western Pacific Ocean with my temporary crew, I stood one watch where the ocean's ship-traffic activity became rather complex and exciting. I was overseeing the geographic plot, and the petty officer assigned to be the plotter was fresh out of school. He understood the theory of how to plot the myriad other vessels in our proximity, the contacts, but he wasn't yet the most efficient at it and he was becoming overwhelmed with the pace of incoming details about bearing, range, and angle of the bow for each of the contacts being identified and tracked. I jotted notes on the incoming data stream for needed plot updates while taking time to explain to the petty officer how to efficiently process the data to portray our situation on the plot. This real-time training put the status depicted on the plot a few minutes behind actual status.

Both the current and incoming COs were in the conning space with us, and the proud CO moved in our direction while saying to his successor, "Let's see what we've got."

Upon reaching our plot, the purpose of which is to depict the full tactical situation, and realizing the depicted status was lagging, the CO looked at me in bewildered surprise and blurted, "Why aren't all contacts shown?"

"I'm training our new plotter as we work. We'll have all contact information updated in a moment," I offered while flushing with guilt.

"What? The geo plot must be kept current at all times," the CO emphasized with frustration and disappointment as he turned away and led his successor toward the sonar shack.

I recognized my error and shifted from teaching mode to operating mode. I gave the petty officer a couple of the more stable contacts to update while I personally plotted those with more dynamic maneuvering profiles. Within minutes, we had the geo plot updated and were able to call the CO and CO-to-be back for their desired update.

I had made a poor decision during that watch. Although the recovery was swift and no harm had come from providing on-the-job training for the green petty officer, the wiser choice would have been to replace the newcomer with an experienced crew member rather than to attempt on-the-job training (OJT) in that environment. Further reflecting upon that situation, I realized that the officer conning the ship, the navigator, the XO, or the CO may have needed the geo plot to help decide the best course for the ship had the scene turned urgent. We were technically in a cold war period, and the geo plot was a key tool for projecting the ship's tactical situation. I had been lucky that the CO's desire to assess the plot when he did was more to admire the skillful positioning of the ship in that congested-water situation than to form a crucial decision on an urgent tactical situation. Not to mention, that deployment was also the departing CO's last run and he had earned the right to make a strong finish. OJT, while important, should have been a lower priority in the given circumstances. I had allowed my comfort in a shipyard training environment to carry over into real peacekeeping operations when I shouldn't have.

Had that poor decision occurred under my permanent duty CO's demanding eye, there would surely have been fireworks. The berating would have been swift, public, and pointed. I would have learned the same lesson but at great cost to crew morale and with a healthy dose of personal embarrassment. In the hosting ship's environment, the CO's reaction was controlled and appropriate. From his question and facial expression, I knew that I had disappointed him, plus I gained a lasting appreciation for the lesson I learned about always being mindful of the operational situation. I have always prioritized the education, training, and mentoring of new teammates, but from that experience onward I have a better appreciation for the proper time and place for conducting OJT.

The Hail and Farewell ceremony between the COs transpired as planned. The deployment had been successful, and the departing CO left on a high note. The formal dress-uniform dinner was an uplifting event, and command of the ship officially transferred to the new CO without a hiccup.

The new CO inspired performance and personal growth. He took the time to learn the personal aspirations of each wardroom member and to offer advice on how to reach those personal goals. Being part of his team, even for a short time, taught me to be a better leader for years to come.

———

In accordance with Article 807 of Navy Regulations, all crew members are present for the formal ceremony marking a change in command. The two that I experienced followed the same general framework. The national anthem played and the official party faced the US flag, with all personnel in uniform saluting. The chaplain gave an invocation, followed by the senior officer making remarks and presenting any decorations or awards being given to the officer being relieved.

The officer being relieved made farewell remarks, read the pertinent portions of their orders of detachment, then stated, "I am ready to be relieved." The relieving officer stepped forward and read their orders of relief, which spelled out the directive from the Bureau of Naval Personnel to formally take command. The new CO saluted the departing CO and stated, "I relieve you, sir (or ma'am)." The outgoing commanding officer returned the salute and responded, "I stand relieved."

In general, if the immediate superior in the chain of command is present, the new commanding officer salutes them and states, "Sir (or ma'am), I have properly relieved (name) as (title of the command)." The new commander then makes brief remarks, expressing pride in the command and wishing their predecessor well, and concluding with "All standing orders, regulations, and instructions remain in effect." They then order an officer to "take charge and dismiss the ship's company." Departure honors are rendered for the official party and the ceremony is concluded. The entire event conveys the formal transfer of authority, and the fact that all crew members and chain of command personnel are present to witness the change in command is paramount to ensure that everyone knows where authority lies.

## LEADERSHIP LESSONS:

**12.A.** Ensure everyone knows who has authority. Leaders and followers alike need to understand who is in charge. Crisp, timely communication to all affected personnel of any changes in leadership is required to ensure smooth operations. This includes not only the obvious changes, such as when a key leader joins or departs a company, but also the subtle or temporary changes, as when the full-time leader is absent or away and designates a representative. Strive to make it clear at all times and among all members of the workforce who is in charge.

**12.B.** Your leadership style has impact. Be aware of your leadership style's impact on others. Study the style and technique of leaders you admire. Make note of those leadership aspects you intend to emulate. Also note the styles and techniques to avoid, those that have less positive or even negative impacts on those being led.

While developing your leadership style, always be authentic. Even if you have witnessed a technique used to great effect by a respected leader, do not attempt to use the approach if it does not feel natural for you. People will sense your discomfort, and the lack of authenticity will hinder your good intent. Also suppress any negative emotion that you may feel welling up when addressing team performance. As noted with the CO's approach, no matter how well-intentioned, a desperate desire for success will induce anxiety within the team and can cause them to perceive you as a demanding stick-bearer rather than a well-intentioned motivator.

**12.C.** Leave a legacy. The truly successful leader can step away while the crew operations continue unaffected. Strive to lead your team in a manner that not only achieves current objectives and delivers on your commitments today, but also that inspires the team to continue performing positively in your absence.

**12.D.** Be mindful of the situation. Assess and be aware of the operational situation at all times to lead at your best. I initially failed to appreciate the distinction between my conditioned training environment and a real situation. OJT is nice when it doesn't get in the way of real-time operations, but it had no place in a live maneuvering encounter. There is not one ideal way to lead; the best course of action always depends upon the situation.

# PART IV

# TRUE LEADER

A true leader inspires others to perform at renewed levels. Where the positional leader relies upon a given title within a defined organizational hierarchy as the basis for authority, the true leader exudes the passion, confidence, and intelligence that motivates others to follow their lead. A true leader offers a refreshing change for subordinates bound by organizational hierarchy to follow a mere positional leader. People are drawn to a true leader, with or without a formal leadership title.

To serve as a true leader is to have a purpose and to be comfortable with decisions, statements, and actions in its pursuit. It is to be authentic. As true leaders, we share a vision to guide our journey, and our passion and confidence inspires others to join in our quest to achieve our objective.

# 13

# SLJO

## LEADERSHIP LESSON 13.A.
## BE INTELLECTUALLY CURIOUS.

My return to PHNSY (Pearl Harbor Naval Shipyard) following the brief sea duty assignment caused me to assess available career paths and various data points along each. The shipyard department heads, those officers who had completed their JO tour and received promotion to the next level of seniority, had each spent their JO tour in a shipyard assignment. The XO and CO, similarly, had spent not only their JO tour but also their department head tours in shipyard commands. Could this be mere coincidence?

A quick study of the fleet wardroom composition in other commands showed that those officers who spent their JO tours at sea went on to department head tours at sea. In keeping with the initial hypothesis, the seagoing department heads ascended to seagoing XO and CO assignments. When a deployed ship ultimately came due for its shipyard overhaul period, the seagoing officers who drove the ship to the yard were soon rotated to other duties and backfilled by officers who had previously served more junior tours in shipyard assignments. The necessity of shipyard time for ships to undergo repairs and upgrades became obvious in hindsight, but it had never arisen in any of the recruiting literature or in conversation with recruiters. There was an unspoken career track of shipyard duty!

Many fine men and women opt for shipyard work. They enjoy the project management work or are energized by the trades—mechanical, electrical, pipe fitting, and so on. They typically are civilians who have selected shipyard work, whether as a career calling or for the financial rewards. Remember the juxtaposition of fresh civilian crews rotating onto the ship every eight hours while their Navy counterparts grew evermore weary standing a 24-hour shipyard duty cycle?

The friendliest of the civilian project managers suggested we go grab a beer one Friday evening. When I arrived at our Waikiki destination, a pub and grill called Moose McGillycuddy's, he was already relaxing with a glass in hand.

"I don't know how you guys can endure those hours. Why did you join the Navy?" he asked as the waitress delivered my drink.

"I needed the money for college. How did you come to be a shipyard PM?" I answered in an effort at commiseration.

"I heard about this gig with high pay, life in Hawaii, and a way to leverage my engineering degree."

His reply seemed a bit too straightforward. "How did you learn the reactor plant systems?" I pushed a bit further.

His response, "The same way you did, in Orlando at NPS," left me momentarily bewildered.

"That's impossible," I countered. "NPS is for Navy personnel . . ."

I caught myself midthought as I had a flashback to the NPS classroom training. There had been a lone student dressed in civilian attire who kept to himself in the NPS classroom, and some early chatter among the JOs about his presence, but we military officers learned not to worry him and vice versa. I suddenly understood the existence of a shadow civilian program whose purpose was to instill the theoretical knowledge base for the civilian shipyard project managers (and that their base pay was substantially more than that of the JO).

Never did I aspire to shipyard work. Someone has to do it, but I'd rather it's not me. At the same time, I'd noticed that officers whose fleet-duty entry point was in a shipyard went on to successive shipyard duty assignments. The trends clearly foretold a future of sequential shipyard tours of duty if I were to pursue a Navy career. The detailer who assigned this young JO to a ship headed into a multiyear overhaul had sealed my career trajectory fate. If there had ever been doubt in my mind on pursuit of a military career, the future choice had now become clear: I would resign my commission as a naval submariner.

## LEADERSHIP LESSON 13.B.
## BEFORE SIGNING A CONTRACT,
## READ AND UNDERSTAND IT IN FULL.

I was struck by another flashback when I naively tried to resign my commission upon completion of my contracted service period.

There was that day back during the training pipeline when I had been pulled from class and presented with paperwork to sign. In recognition of superior performance in consistently graduating near the head of the class with top marks in academics, physical fitness, and military bearing, I was awarded commission into the USN. At the time, I had taken this recognition to be the equivalent of inclusion on a civilian dean's honor roll in college; such recognition is nice but meaningless in the end.

All of us JOs had joined the USN, had we not? Little did I know! Apparently the vast majority of naval officers receive a commission with the United States Navy Reserve (USNR), not to be confused with the regular Navy (USN). By receiving the recognition that day, I was commissioned in the USN. There undoubtedly were perks with this elite commission, but I didn't appreciate them. The clear distinction at this career inflection point was that I was serving at the pleasure of the president of the United

States and would have to request permission to resign my commission! There was no magical returning to life as a civilian upon the end date specified in my service contract. My USN service was to be indefinite—a word which, upon closer inspection, seemed to read but two letters apart from "infinite." The return-to-civilian process required me to submit a formal letter request to resign. The processing time of my request would be one year, and the granting of it was uncertain.

## LEADERSHIP LESSON 13.C.
## CHOOSE YOUR BOSS.

My inquiries into how to draft and submit a USN commission resignation letter prompted a flurry of special career advice sessions with command department heads, the XO, and the CO. These sessions were intended to change my mind, to convince me to remain in the Navy. Their efforts came too late. I had made up my mind and prepared the letter of resignation.

Soon after submitting the formal letter of resignation, I received a special invitation to meet with the fleet admiral, my boss's boss's boss's boss. He questioned my reasoning for wanting to resign. I presented my informal research data on those serving at sea remaining at sea and those serving in the shipyard remaining in the shipyard throughout their naval career duty assignments.

"The career path data I collected makes logical sense. Those with the most specialized skill, knowledge, and experience in a given environment would be expected to most efficiently perform in that environment," I said.

The admiral explained that such is not always the case, that with continued superior performance I could receive future assignments at sea. "Do you think you're smarter than the Navy?" he asked me point blank.

I assured him that was not the case, but that I was able to see a trend and correlate data, and there was only one path that would assure personal control of my career.

## LEADERSHIP LESSON 13.D.
## EARN THE TRUST OF ALL COWORKERS.

My collateral duty assignments changed substantially soon after notifying the Navy of my desired release from service. I quickly learned another military acronym: SLJO, the shitty little jobs officer. No matter the work environment, military or civilian, there are necessary tasks that most people would prefer not to perform. Even at home there are chores such as taking out the trash, washing the dishes, or scrubbing the bathroom that most would forego if given the option. The simple fact is that in order to enjoy the parade, someone will need to clean up after the elephants have passed. Few people aspire to be the one with the shovel trailing the elephants, so shovel duty is often assigned.

Military procedure frequently calls for a double-check confirmation, for tasks performed by a first person to be completed and checked by a second person. To ensure the safety of personnel and equipment prior to commencement of work on a given system, for example, a lockout, tag-out (LOTO) program is in place. One qualified person positions the valves, locks them in the desired open or closed position, and affixes a signed tag on the lock to ensure no inadvertent repositioning of a valve as work is performed on the system. A second qualified person then separately confirms the proper valve positions and lock placement and countersigns the tag to confirm the configuration of the system is as intended for personnel and equipment safety. The double-check process may seem inefficient, but where safety is concerned, the two-person confirmation is unquestionably effective.

In the case of nuclear submarines, not just any person qualified on a system can perform the second check. A qualified officer is required to confirm proper performance of work done by enlisted personnel. In a shipyard environment, with literally hundreds of systems concurrently undergoing various repairs and upgrades, the availability of qualified officers to perform the double-check duties can limit work progress. I became the go-to officer of choice for every SLJ that came along. Someone has to do it, so why bother an officer who ostensibly will serve decades into the future with menial distractions when there is someone who is known to be parting service in your midst? I do not believe there was any intent to haze or punish me for resigning my line officer's commission; it simply would make the lives of other officers a bit more luxurious if I carried the SLJ load. One SLJ assignment too many for someone else might also tilt their thinking in the direction of aspiring to the civilian life.

An especially critical requirement on a submarine is that each confined-space tank be "closed out" by an officer. This requires physically examining the tank volume to confirm that interior conditions are as per specification and that no wrench, washer, nut, or even a single bit of debris remains inside prior to final closeout. For many tanks, this was more of a time sink than anything else, involving a trek up or down to the proper level of the ship to reach the tank's access hole. Some tanks were large enough to require physical entry for inspection; others were too small for full-body entry and required poking one's head in for a look around, aided by a mirror and flashlight. No space goes unused on a submarine, and the tanks located below a walkway deck or behind or above equipment were most interesting to inspect. Accessing these spaces often required wiggling on one's stomach or back, frequently with an arm awkwardly extended to hold a flashlight because the wiggle space was too narrow to later raise a hand from waist to face. It is not a job for the claustrophobic. Teamwork and trust are essential when relying upon another crew member to grab a foot to pull you back out of a confined space, the exit from which is impossible to execute alone.

## LEADERSHIP LESSON 13.E.
## DISTRIBUTE UNDESIRABLE
## TASKS AMONG THE WORKFORCE.

The true test of one's mettle is the internal inspection of a sanitary tank. A sanitary tank sounds like a nice thing, in a manner analogous to an alternative minimum tax sounding like a way to pay the least possible amount of your hard-earned wages to Uncle Sam. Alas, the AMT, though presented as the smallest amount the IRS will extract from your earnings, is a much larger take than you might otherwise pay, and a sanitary tank is the functional equivalent of an outhouse basement. As I donned overalls to head for my first sanitary tank closeout, one of the department heads who knew I enjoyed fishing jabbed, "Don't eat the wrinkle-neck brown trout!" Toilet jokes aside, the duty of closing out tanks would normally be distributed among the wardroom JOs, but as the known commission resigner, the balance of the wardroom enjoyed a free pass while I served out my days as SLJO.

## LEADERSHIP LESSON 13.F.
## KEEP A BALANCED PERSPECTIVE.

Another collateral duty that came with being fully submarine-qualified and on my way out was assignment to be the engineering duty officer during the ship's first steam reentry following the overhaul. The engineering compartment had been in a cold shutdown condition for nearly three years. This was not a reactor startup but an engineering systems' trial period fed by steam produced topside, from the dock. During the overhaul period, virtually every pipe in the engine room had had the lagging removed, replaced, and repainted. Despite the Field Day efforts to keep the engine room in a semiclean state during the prolonged overhaul, there was the inevitable dust deposit to burn away following dormancy. Add to the mix the myriad chemicals of the materials applied during shipyard work that would outgas with renewed energy upon reaching steam temperatures. Anyone who has ever smelled the odor of a home furnace system heating for the winter's first warming will have a vague sense of the experience. Now multiply that odor by a thousandfold. The air during the initial steam introduction became so foul that visibility was limited to mere feet. Our eyes, noses, and throats burned like we had been exposed to riot gas. The effort put forth by the duty crew that night to maintain composure while making rounds and trying to read the myriad gauges and dials through burning and watering eyes was above and beyond the call of duty. I would not wish such an experience upon anyone, friend or foe.

A positive experience of the post-resignation-letter period was assignment as the qualification boards officer. All crew members, enlisted personnel and JOs alike, actively seek qualification for more advanced duties out of desire to become more valuable to the command, to enjoy the increased pay associated with career advancement, and simply out of pride. It was an honor and pleasure to participate on the many qualification boards of eager personnel and to help ensure a positive learning experience for them.

## LEADERSHIP LESSON 13.G.
## LOOK ON THE BRIGHT SIDE.

Another beneficial SLJO collateral assignment was to serve as the submarine's post-overhaul shakedown program manager. Each of the shipyard trades had program managers responsible for confirming proper performance of the many shipboard systems under their purview. I was assigned to schedule the overarching comprehensive tests to be conducted during the ship's inaugural return to sea, the shakedown testing period. There were many hundreds of tests to perform, or in parlance of the day, "evolutions to conduct." Each of the evolutions required specific configuration of various shipboard systems and subsystems for specific time durations at certain speeds, angles, and pressures. These settings had to be exact to collect the required data and confirm passage of a given test.

The shakedown period could last for many weeks or months, depending upon the efficiency and effectiveness of the schedule sequencing, and the results of the tests as they were conducted. To optimize the overall schedule required holistic knowledge of the ship—to understand which tests could be conducted in parallel and which tests required series performance and in what sequence. Efficient scheduling also required knowledge of how much time the crew needs to place the ship's systems into the proper configuration to conduct the next evolution. The most efficient test schedule included the minimal configuration change from one evolution to the next. The three years' experience undergoing shipyard overhaul coupled with the intensive three-month seagoing period had provided me with the in-depth knowledge to provide the most efficient comprehensive shakedown schedule PHNSY had ever seen. Some might consider this experience to be little more than playing 3-D chess; I viewed it as valuable training for transition to large project and program management work in the civilian world.

## LEADERSHIP LESSONS:

**13.A.** Be intellectually curious. And ask the pertinent questions. The civilian in the sea of JOs during Nuclear Power School was a curiosity who could have provided an interesting perspective on the program, had I or any other JO bothered to befriend him and inquire.

Had I truly desired a career of sailing the seven seas, I might have decided at the end of my JO tour to remain in the Navy for a department head tour, an XO tour, and a CO tour of duty. The informal data I collected, however, suggests that I would have been rudely disappointed and denied sea-going tours, being assigned to successive shipyard tours instead.

Learn to ask the pertinent questions and to objectively consider the answers given. Resist the temptation to "hear the answer you want to hear." Instead, strive for an unbiased assessment of the data at hand. When data sets conflict, trust your own judgment.

**13.B.** Before signing a contract, read and understand it in full. It is a common caution to read the fine print. Heed those words and take it a step further.

Read to understand the entirety of a contract. The clause that seems obvious or unnecessary? Ask why it is there. The sentence that seems ambiguous? Have it reworded for crystal clarity. The passage that you do not fully understand but are embarrassed to question? Ask for an explanation! Never assume you know the legal meaning. It is far better to take the time to completely understand the full contents of a contract, even if you feel you are troubling others by asking for clarification, than to leave the door open for a rude future surprise. Read and understand prior to signing any contract. Always.

**13.C.** Choose your boss. When selecting a career option, choose your boss as carefully as the company, the line of work, the work environment, and the financial rewards. Even when all else seems to make this job your dream opportunity, you will not feel fulfilled if you are not well aligned with your boss. Choose someone with whom you feel immediate rapport. Life is too short to toil out of tune with your immediate supervisor.

If you are early in your career, choose a boss from whom you can envision yourself learning and developing. If you are already established in your career, choose a boss with whom you see complementary skills and experiences.

**13.D.** Earn the trust of all coworkers. Even those with whom you do not intend to socialize outside of work. Take the time to build trusting relationships. You never know when you will need to rely on them for help. You may never find yourself dependent upon a coworker to physically pull you from a confined space, facedown, one arm extended forward to hold a flashlight and the other pinned at your waist, as I did when a task required me to wriggle under a narrow walkway. Your job might not involve such ridiculous moments, but nevertheless, you likely will have occasion to wonder if a colleague can reliably assist should you ever find yourself in need. Establish trusting relationships with coworkers in advance of a rainy day.

**13.E.** Distribute undesirable tasks among the workforce. Never consider yourself to be too good for a task, no matter how menial or undesirable. Never assign to anyone else a task that you personally would be unwilling to perform.

Perhaps the SLJO moniker quite literally originated from closing out a sanitary tank? The name's history is unimportant, but the fact that it exists is profound. Take conscious effort to avoid creation of a shitty little jobs role at your place of work. The reality is that undesirable tasks exist in life. In the interest of fair and equitable treatment of employees, go out of your way to evenly distribute the undesirable tasks that no one wants to do. Do not assign unwanted tasks as punishment. Do not assign them to the person who suffers in silence without complaint. Spread the load. (No pun intended.)

**13.F.** Keep a balanced perspective. Someone had to be on duty during the steam reintroduction to the engine room. As a qualified officer with proven systems knowledge and stellar watchstanding record, I was an excellent choice to be on the scene should anything go awry. Assignment as qual boards officer was an honor. I could have viewed it as yet another time sink that took time away from other duties or from my personal time away from work. A healthier view of the assignment was that the ship's leadership appreciated my mastery of the myriad systems, processes, and procedures and leveraged my talents to develop the next generation of upcoming talent. As you step up to the challenges assigned to you, remember that heat and pressure over time turn coal into diamond.

**13.G.** Look on the bright side. Consider how today's experience is adding another brick to your career foundation for future growth. A positive attitude is infectious and will attract others to your cause. The converse is also true; a negative attitude is repulsive and detracts from teamwork. Learn to reframe situations to see the positive and to move onward and upward, brick by brick.

# 14

# MILITARY TO CIVILIAN
# CAREER TRANSITION

## LEADERSHIP LESSON 14.A.
## THERE IS MORE TO LIFE THAN MONEY.

As my SLJO duties drew to a close and my service end date drew near, the
Navy scheduled a course to ease the transition from military service to life
as a civilian. How hard could it be to return to life as a civilian? Had we not
all been civilians prior to military service? To my surprise, the Department
of Defense (DoD) transition course covered a wider range of topics than
anticipated. The comprehensive curriculum touched upon employment
and career planning, relocation planning and assistance, transitional health
care options, and personal finances. Available for further study were bro-
chures on veteran job searching, military skills translation, resume writing
and assessment, calculating a salary, and basic career mapping.

The course instructor provided matter-of-fact data on unemployment benefits, including which states paid the highest rates and how to
apply for unemployment coverage. Rather than sending us "home" to a

member's prior state of residence, all 50 states were presented as potential new home locations to military members transitioning to civilian life. To aid in the selection of a new home state, the instructor provided data on the unemployment payment rates for exiting military members by state. Several of my classmates declared aloud their new affinity for the state with the highest unemployment pay rate.

## LEADERSHIP LESSON 14.B.
## UNDERSTAND ALL DETAILS
## OF THE CONTRACT BEFORE SIGNING.

I completed the basic paperwork that day and requested more information on veteran job searching, which led to outreach from firms that specialize in JMO outplacement. I spoke with two outplacement firms that seemed promising. Their basic business model was to collect DoD information on junior officers exiting the military and to bundle the talent pool information to present to businesses with open positions and an interest in hiring veterans. These outplacement services were free to the individual undergoing the career transition; the firms made their money by charging a finder's/placement fee to the hiring company.

The outplacement firms interviewed me to assess the best-fit potential hiring companies, or so they said. In hindsight, their motivation seems likely to have been to filter for the people deemed most readily employable. The firm I selected, or that selected me, had a curious requirement that I commit to working with them, and only them, for my initial hire out of the military. This exclusivity stipulation gave me pause—I had just learned a lesson from the Navy about understanding the fine details of a contract before signing and had made a personal vow to never again sign away my at-will work rights. After careful study of the concerning verbiage, I realized this JMO outplacement contract clause allowed for cancellation and a move to services elsewhere without a lock-up period; it only required that I work exclusively with them at the time. I signed, still with a bit of trepidation.

## LEADERSHIP LESSON 14.C.
## TAKE A RISK TO EARN A REWARD.

The outplacement services provided by the firm proved to be invaluable. They provided books of required reading on how to prepare for an interview, what questions would likely be asked during an interview, and what clothes to wear to an interview to make the right first impression. They provided resume edit suggestions and even conducted mock interviews, complete with redlines on interview probe responses that they deemed to be mediocre. With their inventory of JMO-soon-to-be-civilians polished for market, the outplacement firm coordinated a forum of hiring companies and JMOs at an accessible airport hotel.

The hiring forum was remarkably well orchestrated. Dozens of hiring companies and dozens of JMO job seekers came together for a cadenced two-day relay of interviews. The companies conducted interviews in hotel suites with candidates from the JMO talent pool that the outplacement firm had selected according to their open search needs. JMO candidates each had a schedule that contained company names, interviewer names, hotel suite numbers, and scheduled interview start and end times. Similarly, each hiring company had a corresponding time schedule with JMO candidates' names and background information. In this format, I interviewed with six separate companies during that single forum, and received six requests for next-level follow-up. The outplacement firm had truly delivered!

## LEADERSHIP LESSON 14.D.
## KNOW WHAT YOU NEED AND WANT
## FROM A CAREER OPPORTUNITY.

I accepted the follow-up requests to visit and interview further with three of the six companies and politely declined the other three. To pursue six opportunities in parallel would have been a logistical challenge, and it seemed only fair to allow the companies of lower personal interest to focus their resources on candidates who were more passionate about them.

Of the three companies I visited for next-round interviews, I eliminated one for the city's terrible air pollution and traffic. In a rental car on my way from the airport to the company site, I could not help but think how awful it must be to live near the ugly brown smog that draped the adjacent hills, and the traffic was a new frustration to me. Upon my arrival, the hiring manager grabbed my hand in a firm shake with palpable enthusiasm and exclaimed, "Welcome to our plant! We're so happy you could make it, and on such a beautiful day with the hills visible in the morning sun!"

"Thank you for inviting me," I replied, trying not to show my astonishment. Really? The smog haze usually is worse than this?

"How was your flight?" he inquired while guiding the way toward a set of interior glass doors.

"It was uneventful. Seeing the sunrise from above the clouds was inspiring," I answered, while thinking the traffic on the drive from the airport was anything but.

The interviews, factory tour, and office visit overall went well, but the harsh reality is that location matters, and in their case, the poor air quality and horrendous traffic surrounding the site were deal breakers for me.

I declined a second company's employment opportunity based on the work content and office environment. The interviewers displayed high interest in me and were excited about their work, but I simply did not share their passion.

"It's great to see you again," opened the talent acquisition manager. "We're looking forward to showing you the campus."

"Thank you. It's great to be here," I acknowledged.

"Let's go meet a key team member, Frank, who's studying to take his PE exam," he suggested while leading our walk along a drab gray aisle between cubicles. We stopped outside a cube where a guy sat slouched over several open engineering textbooks. With two quick raps on the cube frame, the TA manager said, "Jim, allow me to introduce Frank. Frank, Jim is the one I was telling you about. He graduated with an electrical engineering degree from WSU. With honors!"

"It's great to meet you, Jim. I studied mechanical engineering, also at WSU. You graduated in electrical engineering in only four years, and with honors? I'm impressed," Frank opined while shaking my hand.

"Nice to meet you, Frank," was my somewhat bewildered reply.

How odd. I had completed the Navy's postgrad nuke training and had years of experience in the nuclear Navy, yet they were excited about my undergrad studies?

Frank toured me around the facility and provided direct answers to my questions. I had done similar work to what this company did both during my undergraduate studies and in the Navy, but completing it had been required as an assignment, not something that I felt excitement to do of my own free will. The work content and work environment seemed too similar to what you'd find inside a power plant. The interior colors were drab, with few windows to bring in natural light, and the atmosphere lacked the energetic buzz of motivated employees. It was important and meaningful work, but that career fit was for someone other than me.

## LEADERSHIP LESSON 14.E.
## LEVERAGE PRIOR EXPERIENCE.

The third company's follow-up opportunity checked all the right boxes. It would leverage my electrical engineering background, I would be working in a personal hobby area of electronics, they had a high backlog of pending customer orders, and the office was high energy and full of passionate employees. Even the interview questions seemed a perfect fit for me.

"I'd like your thoughts on a recent situation we encountered," Charlie, the interviewer, offered by way of setup.

"Okay," I acknowledged, a bit nervous where this would go.

"We've been having inconsistent performance across equipment bays in the factory. The products are built identically, but they perform differently in the factory," Charlie stated.

"Does one product perform the same way in different bays, or does performance change with the bay?" I asked for clarity.

"No, the performance of a given system changes from one bay to another," Charlie confirmed.

"Have you measured the cleanliness of the electrical power supplied to each bay? I've seen equipment performance fluctuations caused by ground loop electrical signals on the incoming electrical supply lines," I suggested.

"Ha! We just spent two months struggling with the situation before discovering the issue was a ground loop," Charlie replied with a twinge of disbelief and surprise.

During summer breaks from college, I had interned for nascent personal computing companies. One of the internship assignments was to visit the product development labs to determine why test results differed between the lab stations. The same product sample could travel with the same piece of test equipment between lab stations and yield different test results. The product and test equipment pair could return to the various lab stations and deliver consistent measurements, yet the measurements varied between lab stations. My assignment was to determine what caused this aggravating problem.

With a few tables of the possible variables in question, I measured and recorded the pertinent electrical values. The aha moment came when measuring the voltage between "ground" of the standard 120 VAC electrical outlets at the lab stations and actual earth ground. There was up to 60 V potential difference between ground and earth! Troubleshooting that confounding issue in the labs as an intern taught me about ground loops. Flash forward to the third company's onsite interview and the much more educated person across the table describing a problem they were experiencing with inconsistent electrical performance across equipment bays in the factory. The scenario seemed analogous to my internship ground loop experience, which I explained in my response to his inquiry. Yes, this opportunity felt right.

# LEADERSHIP LESSONS:

**14.A.** There is more to life than money. Never allow yourself to be motivated by greed, nor make the mistake of trying to motivate others by purely financial reward.

Seek work and support causes that bring you personal fulfillment, live within your means, and the financial details will become a secondary consideration.

**14.B.** Understand all details of the contract before signing. Yes, you saw this lesson earlier. It is so important that it merits a revisit.

Ask questions. It is better to know for certain what you are committing to than to hope your interpretation is correct and leave yourself vulnerable later on.

**14.C.** Take a risk to earn a reward. Sometimes a bit of risk is required to achieve outsize rewards. Keep an open mind to new experiences. Do keep an eye on the magnitude of risk, however, and the magnitude of the potential reward. The reward must be of sufficient value to justify your taking the risk.

**14.D.** Know what you need and want from a career opportunity. Do not accept just any job offer; search for the right career fit.

As the career advice goes, "Run *to* something, not *from* something." When making a career move, there must be some impetus behind your decision to depart your present role, but be sure also that the new role is a strategic career move that will bring you closer to career fulfillment. Do not simply run from a position in the hopes that the next one will seem better. It may feel good to escape an uncomfortable position, but any career switch is a tactical move. Be sure to make career moves that are strategic in support of your long-term plan.

**14.E.** Leverage prior experience. Bring forth both your experience and knowledge when solving new challenges. Do this while keeping an open mind to new approaches and techniques. By projecting the experiences that brought you to this point and integrating new techniques along the way, you will build a solid path to your future.

# 15

# CIVILIAN APPLICATION OF ELITE LEADERSHIP LESSONS

## LEADERSHIP LESSON 15.A.
## LEVERAGE LESSONS FROM "THE CARE AND FEEDING OF A NEW RECRUIT."

When I started the job in manufacturing as a civilian in the semiconductor capital equipment industry, I knew little about manufacturing and even less about semiconductor capital equipment. My new title, manufacturing engineer III, seemed to imply at least a modicum of manufacturing expertise; I planned to dive into the role with gusto to address the self-conscious gap I felt between title and experience.

As luck would have it, my start date was July 3, which happened to be a Monday, and many of my new colleagues had taken the day off to stretch the Independence Day weekend into a four-day break. The factory had only a minimal crew working, and neither my direct boss nor any other manufacturing engineers were on site. A cordial supervisor in an adjacent department showed me to where he believed my work station would be in a glass-walled, four-person cubicle on the factory floor before sauntering off to attend to other matters. I spent a few minutes checking the desk for basic office supplies and, after locating paper and pen, walked over to the nearest work center to introduce myself to the lady and gentlemen who were diligently assembling electromechanical modules.

## LEADERSHIP LESSON 15.B.
## TAKE ACTION.

The assemblers explained that they were building modules that would be integrated into systems in another work center, which would then move to a final test work center for overall operational and quality checks before being packaged and shipped to business customers as the company's main products. With no specific guidance on what was expected of me, I decided to approach the new role in the manner learned during the Navy's nuclear power training: I would dissect and study each module and subsystem in detail to understand the functions and interconnections between them in order to learn the overall product's operations. I spent the rest of my first day getting to know the skeleton crew on the factory floor, enjoying Q&A discussions with them on their background, their tenure with the company, the name and basic functions of the products they were producing, jotting notes and compiling outlines, and pulling together as much information on product reference material as possible. By the time the full crew returned to work on Wednesday, I was already beginning to speak their language.

My first weeks were self-prescribed 12-hour days of hands-on immersion into product and factory detail. The "half day" work schedule, as compared to my normal shipyard hours, seemed almost a vacation to me, but was deemed silly by fellow MEs and seen as dedicated by management. Although "high-tech" by definition, the semiconductor wafer processing systems we were producing were no more challenging to learn than a nuclear reactor plant when approached in the manner learned at

Nuclear Power School, which is to say piece by piece. To the question "How do you eat an elephant?" a workable response is, "One bite at a time." By studying the subsystem schematics and diagrams, then tracing the physical pneumatic, hydraulic, process gas delivery and electric pipes, tubes, and wires by hand, my holistic, in-depth knowledge of the company's products rapidly grew to eclipse that of any other ME and came to rival that of the original product developers.

## LEADERSHIP LESSON 15.C.
## ENGAGE.

Within three months, I had become the "go to" resource for many of the factory assemblers, technicians, buyers, QA personnel, work center managers, and even senior MEs who had been at the company for years. When a product module or system on the factory floor behaved in an unexpected manner, I was able to suggest most likely causes and, in many cases, was the person to go in and resolve the problem.

When a module test station failed during the last week of the fiscal quarter, panic struck the factory workforce like a plague. The technicians pleaded for help while managers fretted and the ME team said there was little they could do because the test engineer responsible for that particular test station was on vacation out of the country. I volunteered to help and asked that the technicians show me to the ailing test station.

## LEADERSHIP LESSON 15.D.
## REMAIN CALM.

The station looked like an old desktop computer box, with LEDs blinking on the front and cables emanating from the rear. A few questions to the test technicians gave me a general sense of how the test was supposed to be run and how the unit was misbehaving. I removed a few screws and opened the box to find the most impressive wire-wrapping display I had ever encountered. I had heard the term "rat's nest" used to describe electrical wiring before and now understood that it could be an appropriate description. The wire wrapping actually was quite well done, with tidy wraps around each pin of integrated circuit chips, LEDs, resistors, transistors, and capacitors mounted in fiberglass boards. The intimidating appearance drew from the hundreds of wrapped electrical connections, each painstakingly completed with a strand of fine blue wire. The test station innards appeared to be a rat's nest of blue wire encompassing a collection of electronic components. Troubleshooting would have been easier had different circuits been coded by different colored wires, but by carefully tracing individual blue wires from external-cable input, through the internal electronic components, and to the tester outputs, I was soon able to isolate the problem, replace the problematic component, and return the test station to operation.

Back in the cubicle that served as the ME team bullpen a short time later, one of my colleagues commented, "Nice job, Jim! That was impressive the way you calmly repaired the test station."

"Ha! He only seemed calm because he doesn't understand the gravity of the production line being down during the last week of the quarter," was the sarcastic reply from another ME.

"Being on patrol aboard a nuclear submarine when the reactor SCRAMs and you hear the warning 'torpedo in the water' is stressful. Troubleshooting and repairing a test station when no lives are at risk is no cause for panic," I replied to the pair.

## LEADERSHIP LESSON 15.E.
## DOCUMENT PERFORMANCE STANDARDS.

The paucity of technical instructions available for assembling, testing, and troubleshooting the various modules in the factory was a stark contrast to the reactor plant manuals that had been thorough and omnipresent in the Navy. The notes I took during interviews with experienced factory workers, augmented by personal observation and growing hands-on experience with the products, were as comprehensive as any documented reference material being used among the factory employees, so I set about writing procedures to improve factory efficiency and effectiveness. As the assemblers began to follow documented work center instructions, the consistency of the modules assembled substantially improved, which enabled more reliable and consistent performance of the overall systems produced. Within six months of joining the company, management acknowledged my contribution by promoting me to factory work center manager.

## LEADERSHIP LESSON 15.F.
## DISPLAY MUTUAL TRUST AND RESPECT.

As a factory manager, I continued to draw from my experience base, now from both the USN and recent ME work, to drive improvement progress. As a naval division officer, I had the utmost respect for the knowledge, the talent, and the overall value of the machinists, electricians, sonarmen, reactor controlmen, and engineering laboratory technician teams I had the privilege to lead. The factory presented an analogous talent pool of planners, buyers, assemblers, test technicians, and manufacturing engineers. By collaborating with them on the daily challenges as we pursued monthly and quarterly factory output goals, I helped my teams make steady progress on improving shipped product quality and on-time delivery. By soliciting employees' perspectives on the challenges we jointly faced, we established mutual trust and respect and enjoyed new levels of productivity, both as individuals and as a team. The positive work environment perpetuated itself, and through discussing challenges with the team in open collaboration, I found no need to issue a direct order; team members knew what needed to be done, and they took it upon themselves to make it happen. When a bad batch of components arrived, for example, the planner, manufacturing engineer, and buyer huddled to assess the situation. They found an alternate supplier to cover our current need and quickly placed an order to minimize the unproductive time, even while providing feedback to the original supplier of the nonconforming parts to prevent the problem from recurring in the future. After taking these actions, they reported to me on the situation.

## LEADERSHIP LESSON 15.G.
## MAKE USE OF "SPARE" TIME.

On a submarine, there was never an idle moment. When not actively standing watch, there was always another watch station to be studied to further one's overall knowledge of and value to the ship. By learning new systems, taking examinations to prove theoretical knowledge on the new systems, and standing watch under instruction at additional watch stations to demonstrate ability to perform needed watchstander duties, each crew member continually added to his personal qualifications, expanded his knowledge, and increased his value to the team. Why should civilian workers operate any differently? The factory employees in any given work center typically had gained expertise in a narrow scope of work; they seemed content to be experts on a particular module or subsystem, for example. When the backlog of work orders in front of their work center had been fulfilled, those workers tended to either request to build inventory ahead of need, or to cut out early for the day. Neither of these options seemed optimal. Why not learn new skills by cross-training in another area of the factory when presented with idle time? This would increase the factory's flexibility in responding to demand fluctuations and increase each individual worker's personal knowledge and value.

## LEADERSHIP LESSON 15.H.
## MODEL "I DO NOT KNOW, BUT I WILL FIND OUT."

One afternoon, my boss's boss visited the factory to see for himself the progress we had made. I had heard his name and had seen his signature on policy documents from time to time but had never met him in person.

We briefly toured the factory, reviewed the posted KPIs (key process indicators), and headed back to the office for discussion. He gave encouraging words on the obvious progress we had made in quality improvement and on-time delivery of products before asking me for cost-per-unit details. During our tour and conversation to that point, there had been no mention of costs. In fact, never in my time in the Navy nor in my nascent civilian career had I ever been exposed to the financials. Recognizing immediately the gap in my knowledge, I responded to his inquiry with the most valuable answer learned at OCS early in my naval career: "I do not know, but I will find out."

That same afternoon, I sought input from the finance team and began the process of pulling periodic reports of material costs, labor costs, and factory overhead costs that would form the basis of our factory cost KPI. Armed with the preliminary figures, I reported back to the big boss with baseline cost information, in keeping with the "but I will find out" commitment. From that point forward, the fundamental factory KPI set would always include quality, on-time delivery, and cost. The balance of all three is imperative.

## LEADERSHIP LESSON 15.I.
## LEVERAGE THEORY TO PRACTICE.

The Navy's nuclear power training also instilled in me an appreciation for the value of Theory to Practice. Classroom training and studies provide the foundational theory, while actual practice in the plant solidifies that learning in an informed and applicable manner. In pursuit of theoretical knowledge on factory management, I enrolled in courses toward the American Production and Inventory Control Society's (APICS) Certification in Production and Inventory Management (CPIM), which was the standard at the time. The theoretical knowledge I gained through this course of study advanced my appreciation for demand management and forecasting, supply chain management, materials requirements planning (MRP), lead-time management, cost management, and the importance of quality. The classroom lessons and study materials provided a solid base of knowledge for professional materials management that could be applied to the actual business need with only minor modification.

## LEADERSHIP LESSON 15.J.
## ALWAYS BE LEARNING.

I also found the three fundamental pillars of academics, physical fitness, and military bearing, as ingrained in me during OCS, to be applicable to success in civilian life with only minor alteration. Academics I modified to view as the quest for knowledge and continuous learning. Although the real world did not mandate intense courses of study with a rapid cadence of written examinations to prove mastery and retention of subject matter, a self-prescribed study of company literature at a comfortable pace proved invaluable. The study of company products and processes falls into the academics category.

Studying company history, complete with notable business successes and setbacks, provided a solid foundation of knowledge to enable informed communication with colleagues, customers, and suppliers. Learning the jargon and acronyms of the industry, the company, and key customers aided in establishing key relationships. "Speaking their language" makes others more comfortable than expecting them to learn your individual vocabulary or to explain the lingo to you. Keeping current with product changes, new releases, new service offerings, and the problems they would solve for customers became the new norm for success in the civilian world.

## LEADERSHIP LESSON 15.K.
## PRIORITIZE PHYSICAL ACTIVITY.

The second fundamental pillar, physical fitness, is key to good health; we have all known this since an early age. Keeping fitness in mind, I made it a point to exercise regularly and to be mindful of the types and quantities of food I ate in relation to physical activity. Balancing workouts to include aerobic activity and weightlifting helped to keep my overall fitness optimized. Though never one to count calories, I kept in mind how much I was eating in total and tried to eat a healthy, balanced diet. On days when I splurged on dessert, I held myself accountable to do a bit more aerobic activity, whether running, bicycling, or going on a longer hike. If travel or work schedule demands prohibited exercise time for some period, then I compensated by restricting food intake also, especially desserts. The math is simple: Calories in and calories out need to balance over time, unless you're trying to gain or lose weight. Not to mention, exercise reduces stress, which is helpful in both work and personal life. Staying fit improves endurance for those times when the job requires more than eight hours per day or more than five days per week. Staying fit also helps to stave off the inevitable illnesses that circulate through the office or community at large. By maintaining superior fitness, the persistent seasonal bugs rarely took hold of me, and when they did, my symptoms were generally mild. Lower sickness rates translate to less absence and higher productivity at work, and to greater happiness with life in general.

## LEADERSHIP LESSON 15.L.
## PRESENCE IS ESSENTIAL.

The third fundamental pillar, military bearing, I adapted into "presence" for civilian purposes. Being mindful of attire, posture, voice, and word choice, the notion of presence undoubtedly aided my transition to and success in the civilian world. The military prescribed the uniform of the day to be worn; the company dress code was a welcome change to the strict prescription. Even as an individual contributor, with no one under my supervision, I set my sights on joining the ranks of the VPs. Letting the V represent "voice" and the P represent "posture" helped me to project the desired presence in most business settings.

# LEADERSHIP LESSONS:

**15.A.** Leverage lessons from "The Care and Feeding of a New Recruit." The USN produced this educational material, which you can access online, based on lessons learned from woeful missteps in welcoming a new recruit onto an aircraft carrier. Read it and heed it. Similar training should be available to every hiring manager and HR business partner before bringing on a new employee.

**15.B.** Take action. When faced with a daunting situation, size it up, focus on a manageable aspect of it, and begin. To continue the eating-an-elephant metaphor, you can always refocus to another part of the problem if you later learn you were "chewing on the wrong leg," as a cherished colleague would say. The key is to get started and to keep an open mind if priorities change or new information comes to light.

**15.C.** Engage. Seek ways to help. Never shy away from an opportunity to add value. The worst that could have happened when I volunteered to have a look at the failing test equipment is my effort would be for naught and the factory line would remain down. As the saying goes, the only failure is the failure to try.

**15.D.** Remain calm. There is no point in panicking. A bit of adrenaline flowing might heighten performance, but to lose composure and "freak out" adds negative value. In a leadership role, your followers will emulate the emotions that you project, and panic is not a good look.

Reframe the problem statement to a situation that is more comfortable to address, for both you and impacted stakeholders, and approach it with a level head.

**15.E.** Document performance standards. Uniform standards of performance must be documented in writing and readily available to all members wherever consistent performance is desired. When an employee fails to perform in the desired manner, a common cause is poor communication of what is expected between supervisor and worker. Writing down the expected performance standards, along with specific goals and objectives, where appropriate, is a simple way to ensure alignment.

**15.F.** Display mutual trust and respect. Both are essential elements to a well-performing team. You may find that you must go first; use both actions and words to convey your trust and respect in people as individuals. They may have some initial trepidation, but if you consistently provide them the opportunity to demonstrate their ability to perform and provide encouragement rather than negative feedback in the event that they fall short, most people will return in kind with their trust in and respect for you.

**15.G.** Make use of "spare" time. Everyone needs a few minutes' break during the day to clear their mind and make ready for the next matter at hand. When an unexpected white space appears on the calendar, however, make productive use of that spare time. I've found it helpful to keep a list of things that need doing but which lack urgency. When a meeting gets delayed or one ends early, I take a look at my list to see which item might be accomplished in the available time. A perpetual item on this list is walking among the workforce and chatting with a person or two to hear what is really going on and to provide a few words of encouragement. Also keep a list of activities for the broader workforce in the event that idle time falls upon the team at large. Such items as cross-training to learn about new products or markets or performing deferred maintenance on plant or equipment are valuable ways to elevate a workforce in their "spare" time.

**15.H.** Model "I do not know, but I will find out." This is the universal right answer. Whenever you're unsure of an answer, there is no better response. To hazard an unqualified guess can mislead the inquirer, and the basic "I don't know" is insufficient. The key is to honestly admit to not knowing, then to make real efforts to seek out and return the answer at the soonest opportunity.

**15.I.** Leverage Theory to Practice. Understanding the theory behind how something works enables empowered thinking into how that system might be improved. It also supports critical thinking into what can be expected to happen when a variable is changed. Observing the change in actual practice can either confirm your theory to practice expectation or, if the result differs from what you expected, inform you that the theory needs immediate intervention. (Theories are not always correct and may need revision.)

**15.J.** Always be learning. Invest time to understand emerging trends, customer needs, your product and service offerings, and how to make a day in the life of your customer easier.

**15.K.** Prioritize physical activity. Make physical activity a part of your daily routine. There is always time for exercise if you set it as a priority. The benefits are many.

**15.L.** Presence is essential. A quick internet search on "presence" provides the definitions: i) The state or fact of being present; current existence or occurrence. ii) The area immediately surrounding a great personage, especially a sovereign. iii) A person who is present, especially in an impressive way. OCS teaches the notion of command voice. Not a scream or shout, command voice is projected with sufficient volume to command attention, yet in a controlled and confident manner. Using command voice conveys confidence and can help control an otherwise chaotic situation. In the case of a disruptive situation at work, you can use the same command voice principle to clarify the way forward and calm those around you.

As a leader, learn to be subconsciously aware of your presence. Control the tenor and volume of your voice to portray an appropriate presence. Consider the image you are projecting. Dress appropriately for the role you fill, and for the one you seek. Select personal attire appropriate to the occasion that is clean and pressed. If ever in doubt on the dress code for an event, lean to being a bit overdressed rather than underdressed. It is hard to go wrong with showing too much respect for an occasion. Being mindful of posture, whether standing or seated, helps the personal attire selected to project a respectable image. No need to overthink any of these elements, but giving a bit of conscious thought to the details when setting out each morning will help to start the day on track.

# 16

# BEST BOSS

The compliment was an unexpected surprise. I mean, we had been work-ing diligently to deliver on our commitments, all the KPIs were showing trends in the right direction, and it seemed that employee morale was robust, but when the top planner on the team commented that I was the "best boss" she had ever had? Call me surprised. I felt a mix of gratitude, pride, and flattered embarrassment in that moment.

I happened to know one of her former bosses and counted him among the respected leaders from whom I personally had learned. To think that she would consider me in the same grouping as he was flattering; that she would consider me to be performing at a higher level yet was inconceiv-able. After stumbling for a moment on a proper response, I managed to say, "Thank you."

## LEADERSHIP LESSON 16.A
## SHARE CREDIT, TAKE BLAME.

She volunteered that over the past year, she had appreciated the freedom to operate. She felt empowered to do her job. She was comfortable in knowing that I was available to offer assistance or provide guidance should she seek it. She liked that I asked questions to provoke her thinking, allowing her to reach her own sound decisions and to take appropriate actions. She appreciated that I had demonstrated the intellectual curiosity to complete the APICS course of study and CPIM certification to better understand the roles of the team members. And last but not least, she found amazing the way that I shared credit while taking blame. She recalled times when others outside of our organization lauded the value delivered by our team and how I graciously directed the credit to specific team members among us, and times when the external feedback carried disappointment how I personally took full blame as the responsible team leader. Wow. She had given this some thought.

## LEADERSHIP LESSON 16.B
## TO LEAD IS A PRIVILEGE.

As I developed my personal leadership style, a cornerstone was WYSIWYG (what you see is what you get). By being authentic, there was no need to pretend to be something other than my true self. I call this straightforward, no-frills-or-facades style of leadership the true leader approach. Yes, being unabashedly real left me open to eye rolls or snarky shout-downs from other leaders when I would voice an unpopular thought or opinion among the group. The reward far exceeded the cost, however, when making myself vulnerable led team members both to strive ever more diligently to outperform and to increase our mutual trust and respect.

The true leader approach I was taking just seemed right. While listening to senior colleagues speak during meetings, it struck me one day how frequently they spoke of "their" people. Common phrasing was "I had my team do . . ." or "Joe's my engineer" or "Sue's my best planner." Their word choices seemed to imply a sense of ownership or superiority over the teams they led. My perspective was that it was an honor to lead a team, and as much as I felt pride in being a member of the team, the team was not "mine." I certainly felt no possession rights to the team or to any individual member. My conscious effort in actions and words has always been to convey that I have the honor to lead a given team. Every team member serves a particular role; my role just happens to be that of team leader.

## LEADERSHIP LESSON 16.C.
## PRAISE PUBLICLY.

The true leader approach includes an emphasis on open communication. Regular staff meetings are scheduled in advance to address both standing agenda items and timely topics. Standing agenda items include topics such as safety, progress against scheduled team deliverables and commitments, and a review of upcoming calendar events to ensure our collective alignment on team performance. I make a conscious effort during staff meetings to share any thankful comments I've received from external sources since the last session, and to publicly acknowledge the team member or members who delivered the noted value. I also discuss any external feedback received in areas where the team fell short of expectations. Any feedback to an individual for needed performance improvement, of course, is discussed in a private setting, never in an open forum.

Only months after moving to a new leadership position, this time in engineering, it happened again. During one of our regular one-on-one meetings, the top-performing engineer gave me the "best boss" feedback as the reason for productivity dramatically improving across the organization. He cited the new business process flows and empowered work environment. Both happened to be changes that the team had suggested; my role was to recognize the merits of the suggestions and to encourage their implementation.

The third time, shortly after accepting a new role leading a product management organization, a lady with more than a decade's service in that group made the "best boss" declaration. As the glowing feedback accumulated through the various organizations and in divergent leadership roles,

I became more comfortable with the affirmations that the true leader style of leadership garnered.

## LEADERSHIP LESSON 16.D.
## HIRE TOP TALENT.

As team performance grew and broader recognition across the corporation increased, other leaders sought to enhance their own team performance by poaching members from our team. Rather than be perturbed by the loss of a star player, I viewed such moves to be the pinnacle of success. That other leaders recognized the winning performance of our team and coveted the talent we had developed was a rewarding testament to our approach. Our entire team would congratulate our departing team member with a farewell lunch, and I would work with HR to recruit replacement talent.

On every recruitment opportunity, I sought to hire the most promising talent that we could find. My goal was not only to assemble the best possible team but also to bring on board talent that I considered to be a potential successor to my own role as team leader.

One day while eating lunch with colleagues from other parts of the company, a peer leader commented on the success of "Jim's harem." Say again? When I asked for an explanation, he said that people were talking about the all-female team that I had assembled. Others nodded in agreement, as though this was common knowledge. I did not quite grasp the observation, and I certainly did not like the insinuation. Appetite gone, I stopped eating and began taking a mental roster of the current team. Not until that moment did I realize the lead performers in manufacturing engineering, planning, manufacturing supervision, warehouse, and quality were, indeed, all women. Following my practice of hiring the best talent for open roles, those candidates with the strongest backgrounds who were high energy and enthusiastic, I just happened to have hired a roster of exceptional performers who by chance were all female. The team also represented diverse cultures and backgrounds, which was testament to their capabilities rather than any targeted quota.

## LEADERSHIP LESSON 16.E
## DIFFERENTIATE PERFORMANCE FEEDBACK.

My introduction to personnel performance ratings came early in my career with the US Navy. During the 16-week OCS curriculum, we had a cursory review of the Navy's standard evaluation process and form, EVAL, used for annual personnel performance assessment. After the instructor walked us through the various numerical boxes on the EVAL template, we practiced filling out the form by selecting OC peers to review. Knowing that the vast majority of OCs were fresh out of college and had never before written an evaluation of anyone's performance, the EVALs we prepared for one another were primarily for our own practice in how to properly complete an EVAL form. The company officers asked that we try to think of something that differentiated a particular OC from others that we could capture in the freeform text box, letting us know that this peer feedback would be shared with the OC reviewed but that the author would remain anonymous. The resulting EVALs generally indicated everyone across the company was a good crewmate, and some included a specific BZ or two (BZ, or Bravo Zulu, is the naval signal meaning "well done"). An obvious issue was grade inflation; there was no distribution curve of the available 1 to 4 numerical scoring range and so, close crewmates as we were, we all gave scores bunched in the 3.8 to 4.0 side of the scale. Writing nice things about others seemed to come easily for most of us, once we took a moment to consider how teammates added value to our collective performance. We clearly had a wider distribution in performance in reality than the numerical scores suggested—not every one of us truly performed at an outstanding level—but that was not a focus for the EVAL indoctrination exercise.

The next assigned exercise had us selecting a crewmate for practice in writing constructive EVAL feedback. We were to think of something that the recipient could improve upon and convey the essence of that improvement in the EVAL form. Most of us found this second exercise to be something of a challenge. Even knowing the author would remain unknown, we generally found it to be a foreign and awkward assignment to find fault in another member of our company and to write about it in such a way that it would read as constructive criticism. A few examples that came out captured the essence of interpersonal disputes from our early days together, the sort of flare-ups that inevitably occur during the forming/storming period of a new team. The company officer rejected these recollections of disagreements and past grudges and told us to try again with feedback of more substance. The point was to make the recipient of the feedback aware of a potential blind spot or otherwise to provide them with the opportunity to improve in an area that was in some way limiting their potential value to the team.

When annual performance evaluation time rolled around as a division officer responsible for a team of enlisted personnel in the fleet, I recognized the EVAL template from those contrived writing exercises back at OCS. This time was not for practice. The scores I'd mark and the words I'd write would not only become a formal record of a sailor's performance, they would directly impact that sailor's potential for promotion. A promotion to the next rate carried a pay increase. I now had a direct impact on the career and livelihood of the sailors in the division. Fully aware of the awesome responsibility, I spent hours poring over the details, marking the boxes with scores that would provide honest feedback to each sailor, and backed up the numerical scores with considered words. Imagine my surprise when my boss, the department head, tossed the stack of EVALs back and told me to try again. He explained that no one scoring lower than a 3.8 would ever see a promotion, and a score at 3.5 was the kiss of death only given to a sailor whose presence was a disgrace to the Navy. With such system constraints, there was virtually no way to document honest feedback, to differentiate between the rock star performer, the steady-standard performer, and the OBNL (oxygen-breathing no load, the term given to those submarine sailors who did little more than consume the precious oxygen while underway at sea). The Navy has since improved the well-intended but woeful EVAL system that existed during my time, which was fraught with rampant grade inflation.

## LEADERSHIP LESSON 16.F
## PROVIDE TRUE PERFORMANCE FEEDBACK.

The performance appraisal process in the corporate world I found to be much more flexible than its military counterpart. During my first annual performance review cycle as a civilian manager, I once again spent hours summarizing pertinent details of each person's performance. The document format was more a template than a rigid form to complete, and I had ample space to write full details on each performance objective. There was no constraint to thorough description of performance, whether capturing outstanding performance or noting shortfalls and suggesting ways in which the person might boost performance in the future. I diligently drafted a complete, objective, detailed performance assessment for each person on the team and provided the drafts to HR for review.

HR feedback on the reviews I had written was fascinating. The first comment was that mine were perhaps the most thorough and substantive reviews she had ever read. The rock star performers shone from the crowd, the "steady Eddie" (her words) performers would receive positive feedback in areas they excelled while being reminded in areas where they lagged and offered suggested improvement actions, and the low-end performers would receive honest feedback on the need to step up their performance, including outlined improvement action plans. The thing was, HR explained that the low-end performers had generally collected steady-Eddie wording in their prior appraisals. Performance shortcomings I had noted and lower scores that I had marked for the low-end performers had generally been glossed over or absent altogether in prior years' reviews written by former managers.

## LEADERSHIP LESSON 16.G
## BE HONEST TO BE KIND.

Thinking I maybe miscalibrated in my performance review write-ups, specifically with low-end performers, I discussed the expected standards to ensure alignment with HR before sitting down with an employee's prior manager to discuss the perceived disconnects between their prior and my current appraisals. The prior manager laughed knowingly and said, "Oh, him. He's really something, isn't he?" He spoke fondly of the employee, noting how personable he was, always nice in dealings with fellow employees. He noted how the employee had been with the company for many years and had performed for as long as he could remember in the manner conveyed by the performance appraisal I had written. He readily acknowledged the employee's subpar performance and assured me that other former managers would agree. Former managers through the years had wanted to be kind; they were concerned that honest feedback would upset the employee, so they had avoided direct constructive feedback on performance improvement. The employee had been deprived of honest feedback through decades of employment with the company because the managers wanted to be "nice."

I met again with HR to discuss what a "nice" or "kind" leader would do. Would it be nicer or kinder to avoid a crucial conversation and mislead an employee into believing they were meeting all performance expectations when they truly were not? Or would it be nicer and kinder to gently but openly speak the truth to that employee? How would we expect an employee to improve when substantive improvement is needed if we never provide true feedback but instead report that their performance is fine? There is no need to be cold or offensive when discussing feedback with an employee, but the substance shared must be the truth, and the full truth. Each employee deserves and needs to receive true feedback on their performance, even if they might prefer not to hear it.

## LEADERSHIP LESSON 16.H
## LEADERSHIP IS NOT A POPULARITY CONTEST.

Some organizations have no formal performance appraisal system for employees. They might opt not to have a set performance review template to periodically assess and give employees feedback for a variety of reasons. Formal performance appraisal or not, my preferred practice is to meet on a regular basis with each direct report employee. For recent hires onto the team, the cadence might be brief weekly sit-down discussions to address any questions and to ensure the new team member is solidly engaging and finding early traction on key objectives.

For more tenured employees, the cadence is usually a sit-down discussion every second week for a mutual discussion of relevant information. Through these ongoing discussions, the team members are able to keep me current on progress against schedule and business trends, and I am able to provide regular feedback on performance. Any constructive criticism is timely delivered in a private session while accolades and congratulations for successes are announced in team staff meetings and conveyed more personally in one-on-one meetings.

I have carried these practices with me through career moves into new roles across departments, to different divisions within a company, and even to new corporations with great success. To be sure, not every employee immediately embraces the true leadership style. Those who have become complacent "flying under the radar" may not be comfortable with open feedback on individual performance. Others who have become reliant upon top-down communication flow and have become accustomed to waiting to be told what to do would rather not partake in discussions on our collective best course of action. Leadership is not a popularity contest. Some people may resent having to awaken from a too-comfortable state or need help emerging from their shells of reticent withdrawal to step up their performance. Most, however, come to appreciate this inclusive teamworking style after seeing their tentative contributions included in the decision-making process.

Along with the improved team productivity and business success, the most gratifying part of the true leadership style personally is receiving "best boss" feedback from energized employees. This superlative feedback generally comes from top performers on the team. They are capable, ambitious, and enthusiastic, ready to perform at higher levels when given an opportunity with a true leader.

## LEADERSHIP LESSONS:

**16.A.** Share credit, take blame. Whenever possible, publicly recognize team successes. Call out, by name, those individuals most instrumental to achieving the success. Nothing motivates a team faster than basking in the congratulations of a job well done. Even if the particular success is akin to you winning the coach-of-the-year award, recognize that the award is a reflection of team performance, and share the recognition.

Conversely, when the team underperforms, take responsibility for the shortcoming as the team leader. By protecting team players from external negative feedback and taking personal responsibility, the team leader earns tremendous respect. Team members will redouble their efforts to achieve success going forward, not only for themselves but for the leader who represents them.

**16.B.** To lead is a privilege. You are not entitled to be in a leadership role. You own no one other than yourself. Be conscious of your words and actions to ensure that you exude humility, that you remain at all times aware of the privilege you have in filling a leadership role. To speak in "my people" terms is demeaning to subordinates; do not do it.

**16.C.** Praise publicly. Provide constructive criticism privately. People are energized by good news. When the team has earned recognition for a job well done, take the opportunity to share that praise in public. Recognizing the exact individuals who had an outsize contribution to the noteworthy performance not only boosts their morale to continue striving for high performance but also incentivizes others to strive for similar performance recognition. It builds momentum on a virtuous cycle.

Should the team underperform due to a particular team member's shortcomings, never disparage that team member in public or to another employee. In private discussion with the underperforming employee, talk through what happened and agree on a plan to improve performance going forward. Ensure expectations are clear and written out to avoid potential for misunderstanding.

**16.D.** Hire top talent. A true leader should aspire to raise employees' performance individually and in the collective to win, to achieve stated objectives. It follows, then, that as team leader you will strive to lead the best possible team.

When you take over leadership of an already assembled team, your role is to optimize the existing team performance to reach full efficiency and effectiveness. When you have the chance to hire new talent, whether to expand the team or to replace a departing team member, always hire the top talent available. I once worked with an executive whose team was mediocre—on a good day. Most members of his team were low-end performers. After establishing a working relationship and a trusting rapport with this manager, I provided him with a few examples in which members of his team had performed below expectations. He expressed no surprise; he revealed that his intent was to hire people of lower skill in order to justify paying lower wages. He matter-of-factly told me how smart he was for having filled open positions by recruiting people who would accept pay that was below market compensation. As incredible as it may seem, he was proud of the "money he was saving" by assembling an underperforming team! It may sometimes cost a bit more in direct compensation to bring on board top talent, but my experience is that even rock star performers will join at market rates to be part of an outperforming team.

The rush of winning is worth more than a base salary number to the best employees. Hire top talent.

**16.E.** Differentiate performance feedback. An annual performance review summarizes a full year of an employee's life. Set aside sufficient time to provide a complete write-up for each individual. Review the highs and lows of each person's performance over the preceding twelve months and note their contributions to the overall team's performance. Take the opportunity to memorialize specific successes, which will bring lasting motivation to the employee. Also note any significant shortfalls, with specific development actions the employee could take to learn and grow from the miss.

Resist the temptation to write a single generic review for the entire team and do a quick copy-and-paste while changing little more than the employee's name between write-ups. Each employee dedicated a full year to their performance. As the team leader, you owe it to them to provide individualized performance feedback. Show them that you care, that you are aware of their individual contributions to the team's success, and that you support their personal career development.

**16.F.** Provide true performance feedback. Be honest with each employee and tell them the full truth. The employee that is underperforming needs to receive that feedback. It may cause you discomfort writing the words or thinking through what you will say when sitting down to discuss it with an employee, but this sort of feedback is the most important substance. Too many managers shy away from the responsibility and tell a lie of omission; by omitting the true substance from the discussion, the employee is left with the belief that their performance meets all requirements. A true leader speaks the full truth in the service of helping team members perform to their best capabilities.

**16.G.** Be honest to be kind. Do not try to rationalize a reason to avoid having the tough but necessary conversations. The typical alibi that "I didn't want to hurt their feelings" is a weak excuse. If you truly want to be kind, be honest with the feedback that every employee needs to receive. Only by ensuring employees are aware of their true performances can you gift each employee with the opportunity for self-improvement.

**16.H.** Leadership is not a popularity contest. Accept this fact. To release a team's untapped potential, you will need to inspire each individual to perform to a new level. Breaking out of a comfort zone is something most people will not readily do on their own. Some may even actively resist. Being the one to lead the breakout can bring temporary resentment, analogous to the coach who requires athletes to perform conditioning exercises prior to the big game. Lead them to improved performance, however, and most team members will be thankful to have undertaken the journey with you, just as athletes are thrilled after the big game-day win.

# THEMATIC INDEX: LEADERSHIP LESSONS

## GO ALL IN.

**1.A.** Persistence pays.

**1.B.** Commit yourself.

**5.D.** Immersion generates understanding.

**15.C.** Engage.

## BE FLEXIBLE.

**1.C.** Most things in life are negotiable.

**3.B.** Embrace change.

## BE HONEST.

**9.B.** Be honest in your dealings with others.

**11.K.** Protect intellectual property.

**16.F.** Provide true performance feedback.

**16.G.** Be honest to be kind.

## BE HUMBLE.

**5.C.** Practice empathy toward others.

**7.K.** Earn respect, never demand it.

**7.L.** Be vulnerable.

**8.F.** Respect your positional power.

**15.H.** Model "I do not know, but I will find out."

## PAY ATTENTION TO DETAIL.

**2.D.** Read the contract.

**13.B.** Before signing a contract, read and understand it in full.

**14.B.** Understand all details of the contract before signing.

## WORK AS A TEAM.

**2.E.** It takes a team to thrive.

**3.A.** Earn respect.

**4.A.** Teamwork wins.

**6.A.** Communication must be multi-channel.

**8.C.** Engage workers in action planning.

**13.D.** Earn the trust of all coworkers.

**15.F.** Display mutual trust and respect.

## KNOW YOURSELF.

**2.G.** Never confuse "will do" with "can do."

**7.A.** Anticipate your impact on others.

**12.B.** Your leadership style has impact.

**13.C.** Choose your boss.

**14.D.** Know what you need and want from a career opportunity.

**15.L.** Presence is essential.

## PRIORITIZE THE IMPORTANT THINGS.

**4.C.** Wear comfortable clothing.

**7.F.** Keep life's priorities straight.

**8.D.** Make safety the #1 priority.

**10.E.** Put safety as the highest priority at all times.

**11.G.** Protect the environment.

**11.L.** Stretch.

**11.N.** Families matter.

**15.K.** Prioritize physical activity.

## MAINTAIN PERSPECTIVE.

**9.D.** Reframe "problems" as puzzles to be solved.

**9.E.** Sometimes "shit happens."

**11.F.** Maintain perspective.

**11.O.** Less is more.

**13.F.** Keep a balanced perspective.

**13.G.** Look on the bright side.

**14.A.** There is more to life than money.

**15.D.** Remain calm.

## MANAGE TIME.

**4.B.** Manage time.

**5.A.** Forego entertainment television and videos.

**5.B.** Sleep is optional.

**7.D.** Pace the effort.

**10.F.** Leverage 5S+1 techniques.

**15.G.** Make use of "spare" time.

## PLAN AHEAD.

**9.C.** Think ahead to make the most of a given situation.

**9.F.** Communicate intentions before taking action.

**10.B.** Think strategically.

**11.H.** What will go wrong?

**11.M.** $P^7$: Proper Prior Planning Prevents Piss Poor Performance.

## ASSESS THE SITUATION.

**2.A.** Focus on one issue at a time.

**8.E.** Pick your battles and the timing of a confrontation.

**8.G.** Question "the facts."

**8.H.** Assess the situation.

**11.D.** Understand context.

**12.D.** Be mindful of the situation.

## DO THE DIFFICULT THING.

**2.C.** Perform undesirable tasks.

**7.G.** Combat complacency.

**11.E.** Speak up.

**14.C.** Take a risk to earn a reward.

**15.B.** Take action.

**16.H.** Leadership is not a popularity contest.

## BE EFFICIENT.

**9.A.** Leverage existing business assets to boost team morale.

**11.I.** Buy direct.

**11.J.** Set a budget.

## DEVELOP A STRONG TEAM.

**2.B.** Establish an appropriate vetting process.

**10.G.** Plan and care for the new recruit.

**15.A.** Leverage lessons from "The Care and Feeding of a New Recruit."

**15.E.** Document performance standards.

**16.D.** Hire top talent.

## CREDIT OTHERS.

**6.B.** Firefighters are true heroes.

**16.A.** Share credit, take blame.

**16.C.** Praise publicly.

**16.E.** Differentiate performance feedback.

## BE PART OF SOMETHING BIGGER.

**3.C.** Respect those who have gone before you.

**7.B.** Learn from other leaders' actions, both good and bad.

**8.A.** Learn the history of your company.

**8.B.** Consider your impact on the company's reputation.

**10.C.** Policies form the foundation of the work culture.

**12.A.** Ensure everyone knows who has authority.

**12.C.** Leave a legacy.

# GLOSSARY

**1MC:** 1 Main circuit. Primary loudspeaker communication system audible in all spaces throughout the ship.

**BOQ:** Bachelor officers' quarters. The equivalent of a basic hotel on base designated for single officers.

**CO:** Commanding officer. The senior officer responsible for the entire organization. Usually called "captain" by crew members.

**Conn:** Control room area and nerve center of the submarine, located below the sail with ready access to periscope, dive control, sonar room, radio room, and fire control information.

**Cover:** A hat by any other name.

**CoW:** Chief of the watch. The watchstander responsible for trim and drain, masts, antennae, and ventilation.

**Detailer:** The shore-based person responsible for assigning available personnel to duty station needs.

**EAB:** Emergency air breathing apparatus. A face mask with attached hose that must be plugged into one of many air manifolds about the ship to breathe when the environment within the ship becomes unsuitable for unmasked respiration.

**EOOW:** Engineering officer of the watch. The nuclear trained and qualified officer responsible for overseeing reactor plant and engine room operations.

**Field Day:** A thorough cleaning of the ship, top to bottom and side to side. A time to ensure every single item on board is properly stowed in its designated location.

**Geo Plot:** A graphical representation of the surrounding ocean traffic that depicts one's own ship and identified other vessels.

**Grinder:** The marching drill instruction area of OCS; a rough plot of concrete to grind away shoe soles and heels while marching to barked directional orders. Or more pleasantly, a New England–based term for a hero, submarine, hoagie, or otherwise long sandwich of dense, chewy bread.

**Head:** Nautical term for a restroom or toilet.

**HR:** Human resources. The department or persons responsible for employment law compliance and employee relations.

**Jeepney:** Commonly found in the Philippines, a repurposed Jeep vehicle that operates like a taxi or small bus, transporting people along roadways for a small fee.

**JMO:** Junior military officer. Generally the less senior officers, O3 and below.

**JO:** Junior officer. Basically the same as JMO with the "military" being omitted as understood by those in the military.

**Jody:** A cadence call used during training marches to help keep everyone in lockstep and aligned.

**KPI:** Key process indicator. A specific metric of importance to efficient and effective operation. Several KPIs are generally designated for balanced operation of a given area.

**LMET:** Leadership management education and training. A foundational course teaching the four elements titled.

**LOTO:** Lockout, tag-out. A regimented safety protocol that ensures a plant system is in a known, controlled condition prior to conduct of maintenance, repair, inspection, or upgrade. A method to protect personnel and other equipment from release of potential energy.

**MBT:** Main ballast tank. The primary tanks used in buoyancy control of a submarine.

**NPS:** Nuclear power school. An intense six-month course of study in all aspects of naval reactor plant theory and control.

**NROTC:** Naval Reserve Officer Training Corps.

**NRRO:** Naval Reactors Regional Office. Representatives from HQ who drop by ships in port to inspect or audit for proper procedural adherence to all aspects of the reactor plant systems.

**NUPOC:** Nuclear propulsion officer candidate. One channel toward earning an officer's commission. Also, a great way to pay for college and earn supplemental income in school while completing a technical bachelor's degree.

**OBA:** Oxygen breathing apparatus. Another source of breathable air, should the shipboard environment become befouled. Unlike the EAB, the OBA is self-contained to allow for greater mobility. The OBA requires more training in proper use, however, and the wearer must pay close attention to how much oxygen is remaining at any given point.

**OCS:** Officer Candidate School. Where civilians and selected enlisted personnel go to earn their officer commission.

**OJT:** On-the-job training. Hands-on learning acquired by doing the job.

**OOD:** Officer of the deck. The watch officer responsible for all ship activities and control of the watch team as the CO's empowered representative.

**PI:** The Philippine Islands, as spoken by those salty sailors who have made a port call to the Philippines.

**Port and Starboard:** Informal term to describe those assigned to a watch station when only two people are available. Such watchstanders are either on watch or coming from/going on watch. A recipe for sleep deprivation when rotating watchstanding duties in a six-hour shift cycle.

**Rack:** A sailor's bed.

**RHIP:** Rank has its privileges. It's great to be king at the top of the heap.

**SLJO:** Shitty little jobs officer. Self-explanatory.

**SOBC:** Submarine officer's basic course. The studies undertaken by junior officers to learn submarine fundamentals before heading to the fleet on the first seagoing duty assignment.

**TDA:** Temporary duty assignment. As opposed to a permanent change of station, when a military member's talent is needed elsewhere for a relatively short period of time or the assignment is temporary.

**Universal Right Answer:** "I don't know, but I will find out." The right answer to any question, in any setting. Never hazard a guess when unsure; admit you do not know, and then go find the true answer.

**Wardroom:** The assigned dining and meeting space for officers. Also a term used more generally to refer to the officers assigned to a ship.

**XO:** Executive officer. The second in command under the CO who will assume responsibilities for the command, should the CO become incapacitated.

**YoYo:** Quick change of uniform from one set of regulation garb to another (e.g., khakis to blue or whites). Perhaps an acronym for "you're in, you're out" of a specific uniform?

# ABOUT THE AUTHOR

**JAMES L. BARNHART,** a Distinguished Naval Graduate of the US Navy's Officer Candidate School, served as a naval engineering officer leading nuclear controls and instrumentation divisions aboard submarines. Jim built upon his foundational nuclear Navy experience in the corporate business arena to enable business customer delight through flexible and industry-leading services and operational excellence during hypergrowth periods for start-ups and established companies.

Recognized for his distinguished C-suite career developing winning teams, advancing global growth, delivering record financial performance, and earning best-in-class customer satisfaction with superior operational performance, Jim is pursued as a speaker and advisor.

Jim holds a BS in electrical engineering from Washington State University and an MBA from Haas School of Business at UC Berkeley.